RIGHTEOUS REVENGE

GETTING DOWN TO GETTING EVEN

GEORGE HAYDUKE

A LYLE STUART BOOK
Published by Carol Publishing Group

Also by George Hayduke:

Getting Even
Getting Even II
Mayhem
Make'Em Pay!
Make My Day!
Advanced Backstabbing and Mudslinging Techniques
Revenge!

Righteous Revenge:
Getting Down to Getting Even
by George Hayduke

First Carol Publishing Group Edition 1993

Copyright © 1991 by George Hayduke
All rights reserved. No part of this book may be reproduced in any form, except by a newspaper or magazine reviewer who wishes to quote brief passages in connection with a review.

A Lyle Stuart Book
Published by Carol Publishing Group
Lyle Stuart is a registered trademark of Carol Communications, Inc.
Editorial Offices: 600 Madison Avenue, New York, N.Y. 10022
Sales and Distribution Offices: 120 Enterprise Avenue, Secaucus, N.J. 07094
In Canada: Canadian Manda Group, P.O. Box 920, Station U, Toronto, Ontario M8Z 5P9
Queries regarding rights and permissions should be addressed to Carol Publishing Group, 600 Madison Avenue, New York, N.Y. 10022

Published by arrangement with Paladin Press, Boulder, Colorado

Carol Publishing Group books are available at special discounts for bulk purchases, for sales promotions, fund raising, or educational purposes. Special editions can be created to specifications. For details, contact Special Sales Department, Carol Publishing Group, 120 Enterprise Avenue, Secaucus, N.J. 07094.

ISBN 0-8184-0569-4

Manufactured in the United States of America

10 9 8 7 6 5 4 3 2 1

Neither the author nor the publisher assumes
any responsibility for the use or misuse of
information contained in this book.

CONTENTS

Introduction 1
General Advice 9
The Eleven Commandments of Revenge 13
How to Use This Book 16
Caution 17
Anatomy 19
Answering Machines 22
Automobiles 25
Balloons 32
Bankcards 34
Bar Bands 37
Boats 39
Bombs 41
Bugs 43
Bullies 46
Bumper Stickers 49
Cable Television 51
Car Dealers 54
CB Radios 58
CIA 60
Computers 62
Credit 66

Credit Cards	68
Deadbeats	70
Doctors	72
Dope	74
Fire	78
Fish	80
Food	82
Formulae	84
Funerals	87
Gifts	89
Graffiti	91
Gun Grabbers	94
Halloween	96
Hijacking	99
Home	101
Hookers	104
ID Cards	107
In Privity	109
IRS	111
Jail	113
Jocks	115
Junque Mail	117
Kiddies	120
Landlords	123
Laundry	126
Mail	128
Mark	130
Military	133
My Slogan	136
Neighbors	137
Nuclear	139
Office	141
Party	143
Pets	145

Photography	147
Plants, Gardens, & Lawns	149
Police	151
Poop	154
Porno	158
Posters	163
Quotes	164
Radar	168
Radicals	170
Roadkill	172
Schools	175
Sewage	180
Sex	183
Skateboarders	187
Smokers	189
Sources	191
Stores	199
Sweeties	202
Telephones	206
Telethons	210
Television	212
Trash	215
Urine	217
Utility Companies	219
Vermin	221
Video	223
Vomit	225
Xmas	227
The Last Word	229

I'M HONORED

For once I am almost ego-struck with speechless modesty. Someone wrote a nice poem about me. It came by way of Biggus Piraphicus and was written by his good friend Belzebubba. I know I've heard that name somewhere. Was it in *Ghostbusters,* or did I really read it on an archaeological ruin in the South Bronx?

Here is Belzebubba's poetry in my honor:

ODE TO GEORGE HAYDUKE
by Belzebubba, Texas, 1989

I'm not going to take it anymore.
I've bought Hayduke's books.
He's shown me the way.
For, pay, shall the crooks.

There stood George, inspired revenge master,
Put stuff in a gas tank, like money in the bank.

Condom with mayo
Appeared in another's purse.

You know she's the kind
Who'd tailgate a hearse.

Scuzzy porno books
Appeared in mark's briefcase.
When it opens it up
Red turns his face.

Potato in a tailpipe
Damaged a garage door
Now she's no longer his paramour.

Hey there, Georgie boy,
You strike terror in their hearts.
And the famous flaming towel
Butchers the sacred cow.

Costing many $$$
To repair his deeds
To bite the hand that feeds
To get your mark's back.

OK, so it won't make the *Harvard Literary Review*, but then, neither will I—and it is the only poem I've ever had. I'm touched. I should set the words to tune and do a music video. I could call it "Handel with Care." And, that would really get me on somebody's Black Liszt.
I quit.

FOR FUN

These two gutsy, erstwhile explorers, no doubt Sackett-like men such as Peder Lund, Paco Escobar, Larry Grupp, or Bob Brown, were in the wilds of East Los Angeles when a ferocious lion jumped right out at them.

"Keep calm," whispered the first. "Remember what we read in our manuals and books about this sort of thing."

"Right," said the second. "Stand still and tall and look the bastard in the eye. He'll turn and run.

"I was just thinking, though, what if the lion hasn't read the same books we have?"

Credit for the fact that you're reading this book, beyond that due Squire Lund, goes to Travis Kenneth Bynum and Tom Johnson, two of the most dangerous philosophers I've met recently; to Ambrose Bierce and Major Amos Hoople, bless them; to Marie L. and the Amityville Horror; and, of course, to Maugie, whose thoughts I found fun and fulfilling, and whose memory reminds me to add ". . . to absent friends."

INTRODUCTION

A member of our beloved U.S. Department of Just Us told me indirectly that government officials not only do not approve of my books, they want them to be banned. Hence, I was very flattered when several of U.S. Attorney General Richard Thornburgh's secret police tried to entrap yours truly in 1990 with a nasty little scam.

Probably because he's been so busy building the new American police state, Thought Control Czar Thornburgh has never read Alfred Whitney Griswold, who once noted, "Books won't stay banned. They won't burn. Ideas won't go to jail. In the long run of history, the censor and the inquisitor have always lost. The only sure weapon against bad ideas is better ideas. The source of better ideas is wisdom. The surest path to wisdom is a liberal education."

Part of that liberal education involves reading books, all sorts of books, and exploring new ideas.

I write these books because I value liberty and freedom. I love freedom and liberty. I fought for liberty and freedom. But, I get very sad when I see what is being done to our wonderful country.

In Las Vegas recently, after looking around the rabble, fellow Paladin author Bob Burton (*Bounty Hunter* and *The Bail Enforcer*) turned to *Soldier of Fortune* magazine publisher Bob Brown, Paladin publisher Peder Lund, and me, shook his head, and muttered, "Our great nation has become a land of car-wash laborers ruled by reserve corporals and clerks." I told him he had forgotten the third leg of this repugnant troika, the career creeps that fewer and fewer of our citizenry perennially re-elect.

It frightens me how readily our fellow citizens give up their freedoms to our burgeoning police state. The police state sets roadblocks to stop our cars and check for drunk drivers, drugs, or firearms. Probable cause and reasonable doubt have no place on the police-state agenda. What's next for our political Gestapo: books, ideas, thoughts?

Hey, I'm serious. Just recently, for the first time since I began writing these books, I ran into censorship from timid media people who fear the wrath of the moral zealots of the religious/political right wing of the Republican party.

Back in 1980 when I found out that writing these books grabbed the attention of radio talk-show hosts, I discovered that I was a glutton for this sort of ego-stroking. I love doing talk shows and have established some solid professional friendships with radio folks in cities all over the United States, Canada, Australia, Germany, Mexico, and elsewhere.

I've had a ball, especially on the North American talk shows, sharing hundreds of laughs with fun people in such fun places as Beaverlick, Manitoba; Dumptown, Ohio; Beerphart, Idaho; Codger Corners, Arizona; Biblebreath, Georgia; Dismal Seepage, New Jersey, and so on and on and on.

My first censorious experience came on November 1, 1988, when some brainfart named Gary Dee stood me up on a scheduled appearance for WWWE radio in Cleveland because he disapproved of my books. He didn't think they were funny. No problem. But, why did this *Kuhscheiss* of the airwaves ask me to be on his show if he was so terrified of my humor seeping through to the minions of Cleveland? Gary's toady assistant mumbled a wimpy apology for not allowing me on the air and hung up.

Then, a year down the road, I landed in another world: Harrisburg, Pennsylvania. Harrisburg is inhabited by backward, ill-humored, beetle-minded curmudgeons, many of whom, rather frighteningly, are also breeding stock. It's also the only market in which I've gotten more than one or two negative calls. The rest of the listeners were far enough up the food chain to realize my act is satire, humor, a joke.

I later asked The Big Kahuna, a scholar who's studied that area for some years, for his reading of Harrisburg. He laughed and mentioned inbreeding and Mendel's experiments with garden peas. His lovely wife, Merry Annie, an astute observer of the contemporary scene, told me, "You see, Harrisburg is the seat of state government in Pennsylvania, plus Three Mile Island is also here. Everyone blames Three Mile Island for everything. However, that's not the case. It's the proximity of the state legislature that causes all the residual backwardness, asininity, and dullness."

With that in mind, I shook off my malaise and recalled wonderful radio interviews in Indianapolis, West Palm Beach, Phoenix, Denver, South Bend, Atlanta, Chicago, Vancouver, and other places where the audience and I had shared many laughs and hoots.

By the way, in case you're watching that TV show business euphemistically called news and someone asks you what they call that silly business of newscasters stacking and restacking their scripts at the end of the show, it's called *revulipulancy*. You can thank former network newsman David Hazinski for that bit of arcanum.

The most inane, hypocritical, and disgusting nest of vermin available, American Politicians for the '90s, tried to rape the Constitution because some asshole burned a cloth replica of the U.S. flag. That replica flag is the symbol for the very freedom that allows some mouse fart to destroy it. That principle, dear friend, is far more vital to America than another police state mandate.

However, in the spirit of compromise, I guess it might be all right to attack, kick, burn, punch, beat upon, or pummel a flag replica if a politician has wrapped itself in one.

Then there are the gun-control dipshits who feel that if guns are banned, violence and crime will go away. This foolishness is cheered by the majority of Big Media Mavins, most of whom openly admit their bias and agenda. I won't waste my paper or your time refuting that nonsense. Remember the gun-control cowardice and the elections of 1990 . . . do something about it.

Please, gentle reader, don't let them take away any more of our constitutional rights and freedoms. Remember, when people are both overtaxed and overregulated, there is little freedom to be found.

How far are we from the words spoken at Auschwitz by *SS Hauptsturmfuhrer* Dr. Josef Mengele, who would fit right in with the U.S. government's professional police state, "Here the Jews enter through the gate and leave through the chimney."

The meek will never inherit our savage Earth, which is sad because the meek are probably the most civilized among us. The truth is, they need their own savages to fight for them, to help them push back the Huns and the Philistines. I subscribe to the World War II axiom of Admiral Ernest King that when things get really bad, send for the real hard-nosed sons-of-bitches. That's what Haydukery is, folks—being bullybusters for the little folks.

When asked for a one-line summary of what Hayduking is all about, I reply that it is about being tired of some schmuck pissing in your face, then having to thank Mr. Schmuck for selling you a towel to wipe his piss off your face.

Don't be a nebbish, a victim afraid to strike back at the bullies and villains who torment your life. William Shakespeare characterized too many of us when he wrote, "Life's but a walking shadow, a poor player that struts and frets his hour upon the stage, and then is heard no more."

Alfred Hitchcock brought us the concept of the MacGuffin, which is an object, prize, or perhaps an achievement that entices people to cross almost any moral or physical border to obtain it. In a sense, then, hitting back at their tormentor could be considered a MacGuffin for many folks.

A good-natured, intelligent gent named Andrew once sent me a letter that had been typed on the back of a National Rifle Association (NRA) pistol target. Although he was still indentured to our military's officer corps at the time, Andrew was (and is) a good man. Andrew shared some philosophy that brought me both to tears and laughter. In the spirit of karma, I will share it with you:

> "I will observe nature in all her glory, seek understanding with our Creator, hallucinate a bit, and entertain myself with thoughts of feeding a grizzly bear a bucket of raw meat laced with peyote buttons, then setting him him loose to a packed house of congressmen and lawyers . . . I once had a wonderful dream of the Reagans fleeing a pack of homeless, rabid white poodles . . . They were forced to take refuge in a toxic-waste dump managed by James Watt and Edwin Meese."

That's a wonderful MacGuffin for all of us.

◆

I don't know. Maybe all of my concern about our freedoms is just a wild, rowdy carnival in the national colon, and maybe there is nothing to the fact that lawyers in Washington are walking around these days with their hands in their own pockets instead of ours.

And, it's also possible that Maggie and Denis Thatcher will be seen barhopping in Tijuana and Nogales along with Dan and Marilyn Quayle. All of which is about as likely as Ollie North getting hired as a towel boy in a gay bathhouse owned by Edwin Meese. Oh well, nobody's ever going to mistake me for a rising young archbishop working his way up the corporate ladder of Mother Church, either.

Perhaps there are more important issues for our time than this erosion of our freedom. For example, I have spent hours wondering where your lap goes when you stand up. If it rains in a rain forest, what happens in a petrified forest? Would you rather walk to work or carry your lunch?

I hope you like this book. Read it in good fun and enjoy the laughs. After all, the second reason I write these books is to entertain you, wagging my tongue at my long-dead high-school teacher who told me I'd never have any success as a professional class clown. Before turning to the next page, though, join me in a toast.

The first time I heard this classic toast was from an old sergeant major I'd come to know well and to respect even more. As we had our final lemonade together he told me, "May all your friends be old and all your wars be cold."

George Hayduke
Pizda, Surinam
November 1990

GENERAL ADVICE

Throughout this book, I make universal reference to the "mark," which is a street label hung on the victim—male or female—of a scam, con, or act of vengeance. In our case, the mark is a bully—anyone or anything—who has done something unpleasant, foul, or unforgivable to you, your family, your property, or your friends. Never think of a mark as the victim of dirty tricks. Think of the mark as a very deserving bully, a target of your revenge.

Before you study any of the specific sections of this book, read these vital paragraphs. They tell you how to prepare before going into action.

1. *Prepare a plan.* Plan all details before you take action at all. Don't even ad-lib something from this book without an exact plan of what you're going to do and how. If your campaign involves a series of actions, make a chronological chart (don't forget to destroy it when you're through) and then coordinate your efforts. Make a list of possible problems.

Plan what you'll do if you get caught —depending upon who catches you. You must have every option, contingency, action, reaction, and evaluation planned in advance. Remember, time is usually on the side of the trickster. As Winston Churchill, one of my favorite heroes for many, many reasons, once said, "A lie gets halfway around the world before the truth gets in its boots." Or, as that old Sicilian homily goes, "Revenge is a dish best served cold," which means don't strike while your ire is hot. Wait. Plan. Think. Learn.

2. *Gather intelligence.* Do what a real intelligence operative would do: compile a file on your mark. How detailed and thorough you are depends upon your mark. For a simple get-even number, you obviously need less inside information than if you're planning an involved, time-release campaign. Before you start spying, make a written list of all the important things you need to know about that target—be it a person, company, or institution.

3. *Buy away from home.* Any supplies, materials, or services you need must be purchased away from where you live. Buy far in advance and pay in cash. Try to be as inconspicuous and colorless as possible. Don't talk unnecessarily with people. The best rule here is the spy's favorite: a good operative will get lost in a crowd of one. The idea is for people not to remember you.

4. *Never tip your hand.* Don't get cocky, cute 'n

clever and start dropping hints about who's doing what to whom. I know that may sound stupid, but some would-be tricksters are gabby. Of course, in some cases, this will not apply, e.g., unselling car customers at the dealership or other tricks in which the scenario demands your personal involvement.

5. *Try to make your punishment fit the crime.* Just as in Sir William Gilbert's poem, which Sir Arthur Sullivan set to music and called *The Mikado*, your punishment should fit your mark's crime. One benefit is that the irony may not be wasted on the mark. Another is the humor you will realize. After all, it's the same old biblical eye-and-tooth stuff.

6. *Never admit anything.* If accused, act shocked, hurt, outraged, or amused, whichever seems appropriate. Deny everything, unless, again, your plan involves overt personal involvement. If you're working covertly, stay that way. The only cool guy out of Watergate was G. Gordon Liddy, who kept his mouth shut.

7. *Never apologize; it's a sign of weakness. Besides, they can't prove anything.* Normally, harassment of a citizen is a low-priority case with the police. The priority increases along with the mark's socioeconomic status in the community and his or her political connections. If you are at war with a corporation, utility, or institution, that's a different ball game. They often employ private security

people, sometimes retired federal or state investigators. By habit, these people may not play according to the law. If you play dirty tricks upon a government body, prepare to have a case opened. But how hard it is pursued depends upon a lot of factors. Understanding all this ahead of time is part of your intelligence planning before you get started.

THE ELEVEN COMMANDMENTS OF REVENGE

Thanks to my Apostle of Revenge, Dick Smegma, I humbly present for your perusal, belief, and adherence the Eleven Commandments of Revenge. Stay faithful to them and you'll enjoy a lot of yucks without suffering the heartbreak of being caught.

1. *Thou shalt neither trust nor confide in anyone!* If you do, that person could eventually betray you. Even if it is a relative or spouse, don't tell anybody what you are up to. Implicated accomplices are OK.

2. *Thou shalt never use thy own telephone for revenge business!* Always use a public telephone or that of an unwitting mark so calls cannot be traced back to you or to someone who knows you.

3. *Thou shalt not touch revenge documents with thy bare hands!* Bare hands leave fingerprints. Wear gloves.

4. ***Thou shalt become a garbage collector!*** Once your victim places his trash outside his home or office for pickup, it is legal for you to pick it up yourself. You can learn a lot about your mark by sifting through his papers and such. The pros do it all the time.

5. ***Thou shalt bide thy time before activating a revenge plot!*** Give the victim time to forget about you and what he's done to wrong you. Getting even too soon makes it easier for him to discover who's doing it.

6. ***Thou shalt secure a "mail drop" address in another city!*** You don't want revenge mail being traced back to your residence/home, do you?

7. ***Thou shalt learn everything there is to know about thy victim!*** The best revenge schemes or plans are hatched by people who know their victims better than their victims know themselves.

8. ***Thou shalt pay cash all the time in a revenge plot!*** Checks, money orders, and other paper transfers can be traced back to you. Cash cannot.

9. ***Thou shalt trade with merchants who have never heard of you!*** Do business with people only once when involved in a revenge plot. You can wear a disguise so the people you are involved with will have trouble identifying you in a legal confrontation.

10. ***Thou shalt never threaten thy victim!*** Why warn your intended victim that you are going to get even? When bad things begin to happen to your victim—whether or not you caused them—your victim will remember your threat, and he or she will set out to even the score with you.

11. ***Thou shalt not leave evidence lying around, however circumstantial!*** If you are thought to be actively engaged in having fun at your mark's expense, the authorities may visit you. Thus, it would be prudent not to have any of my books at home or in the office. Note well what Francois de La Rochefoucauld wrote in *Maximes*, "The height of cleverness is to be able to conceal it."

HOW TO USE THIS BOOK

I have arranged these subjects by method and mark, listing them alphabetically. In addition to using the obvious subject headings, you can also do a cross-reference of your own. Or you can adapt a method listed for one mark to another mark or situation. This book is as versatile as your own imagination.

While this mix 'n' match versatility is standard, the personalized nasty touch is still the best. Another effective part of this business is the anticipation of further damage after your initial attack. This is grand psychological warfare.

This entire concept reminds me of what Ralph Waldo Emerson wrote about a weed, "And what is a weed? It's a plant whose virtues have not yet been discovered."

CAUTION

The schemes, tricks, scams, stunts, cons, and scenarios presented here are for information and amusement purposes only. It is not my intent that you use this book as a manual or trickster's cookbook. I certainly don't expect that anyone who reads this book would actually ever do any of the things described here. This book is written solely to entertain and inform my readers, not to instruct or persuade anyone to commit any unpleasant or illegal act. Given my own mild disposition, I could hardly tell someone else to make any of these tactics operational.

Consider the case of mistaken vengeance that took place in Vienna, Austria, in 1985, when Leopold Renner thought his wife was cheating on him because he saw her holding hands with another man. The shocked husband stuffed twenty-seven of her live exotic pets—one after another—into the churning garbage disposal. Down went screaming parakeets, hamsters, mice, and tarsiers into a gushy gruel feeding into the sewage drains.

Fact: His wife, Frieda, had been holding the hand of her brother, whom she had not seen in a dozen years, and she was bringing him home to meet her husband. True story.

A good Hayduker works smart and covers all of the angles. Plan for all options and all contingencies. And remember this worthy advice from J.R.R. Tolkien, "It doesn't do to leave a live dragon out of your calculations if you live near him."

If you're going to kick over an anthill, do it fast and right the first time and don't get your boot stuck, or the ants will eat you alive. Ahh, that's meant as an analogy, of course. Likewise, you don't go hunting vampires without making certain you have garlic, a cross, plus wooden stakes and a mallet.

Yes, caution is important. Don't take a foolish or stupid mark lightly. Personally, dangerous fools frighten me more than clever enemies. Remember that old Shinto proverb that a nest of vipers is not as deadly as one hungry man.

Finally, some readers will be outraged by my attitudes, language, and view of our systems, people, and institutions. I do not see our world through the same rose-colored glasses that they do. My glasses are jaundice-colored. If my language, ideas, and philosophies offend you, remember, gentle reader, that vulgarity is the garlic in the salad of taste.

ANATOMY

Leave it to Prairie Dog to teach this old revenge hound a new trick. At the height of the popularity of those stupid, yellow, triangular message plaques that Muddle Americans plastered in their cars, e.g., Braindead on Board, Prairie Dog wanted something original.

"Also, George, out my way, there'd been a lot of middle-fingered salutes and overall bad manners," Prairie Dog told me.

Prairie Dog took a Nerf football and cut it in half. He mounted each half lengthwise on a small wooden panel a tad larger than the football halves. He glued a handle to the other side of the panel.

Next, he painted each half flesh-colored. Then, he took an old pair of pants, cut two inches down from the waistband, and glued them to the board just at the bottom of the "ass." A similar facade of a shirttail at the top completed the project.

To activate this artificial moon, you just hold the handle and press the cheek side firmly against your car, bus, van, or train window. You could also use this in a classroom, studio, apartment, house, or hospital.

As Prairie Dog reported, "It's hilarious to see people's expressions, wondering how you can drive and still moon them, or what other people on the bus must think. It looks that real."

Good stunt, Prairie Dog. Bet you, gentle reader, Nerfer thought the moon wouldn't be a balloon.

◆

You'd like my friend Ella Valet. She's gentle, kind, totally gorgeous, and very strong in many ways. She also has a honed sense of twisted humor, which she used to help keep a true nasty away from a friend's daughter.

Ella said, "Let's call this knave King, which he thought he was, even though he was a slime. I'll not even begin to dredge the awful things he did to poor Lisa, the victim. But, we paid him in full."

King traveled often and was careless about leaving his documents out. Ella arranged for a friend in another country, which shall remain nameless for now, to visit King in his room, using some winning ways to gain his attention. While he was occupied getting refreshments, Ella's friend managed to stamp "Deceased" on every page of his U.S. passport with a close replica of the official stamp for such activity.

Although King was disappointed, Ella's friend left without compromise or incident. Happily,

King was both and more. His stay in this foreign country was compromised, incidental, inhospitable, extended, and costly.

ANSWERING MACHINES

She was another K-Mart Mother for Moral Mediocrity, one of those religious yahoos with a white ribbon on her car antenna, a contribution of one hundred dollars each week for a slick televangelist, a dead spot for Elvis in her heart, and an atrophied G-spot in her apathy. She also made Misfit's life miserable by her loud and constant preaching, screaming, and proselytizing of everyone in the neighborhood to her fundamental madness.

Well into the night, Misfit could hear loud religious music, chants, prayers, and talking in tongues coming from her place. "But, enough was enough," Misfit said, "when she got this answering machine that played prayer stuff back at me when I called her at midnight to ask her to quiet down."

Misfit hooked up his own cassette recorder and recorded the Holyhell Lady's message . . . twice. He then called back and, at the beep on her machine, played back the tape of her outgoing message, repeated, of course.

"I understand she was at the local electronics store three or four times about the 'problem' with her machine. I waited a few weeks, then did it again. It always worked well at random times."

◆

Tyra Pierce is back with us again, this time with an amusing story about how someone he knows got even with a nasty professional person who liked to bully elderly folks. It seems that this bad guy had one of those fancy machines that allowed him to call in and check his messages, plus change the outgoing message, all by remote control.

To have some fun with this, according to Tyra, all you need is the access code, which does not vary much from machine to machine in this product line.

"I had a friend visiting from out of town, and on a pretext, I had him check in the mark's office for information. While chatting informally, my friend told the secretary he was interested in buying a new answering machine for his office and was asking people how they liked theirs when he was in other offices," Tyra related.

She let him look at Mr. Mark's machine. Tyra's pal casually looked it over, memorizing the brand and model. His next stop was an electronics shop. Tyra's pal told the clerk the instruction manual was missing from the machine he'd bought earlier that week. He offered to pay if the clerk would make a photocopy of the booklet from another machine.

Armed with this booklet, which included four possible access code options, Tyra waited for five weeks so the casual visit of his pal to Mr. Mark's office would be forgotten. He then began thinking of how to change some of the outgoing messages on his mark's machine. Here are some of the samples he considered implanting on the machine for outgoing messages:

- "Hi, this is Mark. Is that a cigar you're smoking, or do you have a dog turd in your mouth?"
- "This is Mark. Don't ever call here again, because your breath smells like a stale rhino fart (or a human death fart)."
- "Hello, this is Mark. Don't ever call here again, or I'll come to your place and shit down your throat."
- "Hi, Fuckface, this is Mark. If your IQ gets any lower, we're going to have to water you twice a day."
- "This is Mark. Look, you prissy asshole, if you ever call here again, I'm going to come over there and sit on your face."
- "This is Mark. I can't come to the phone now because I'm having (graphically describe some specific deviant sexual stunt) with my (secretary, child, grandchild, family pet, your spouse . . . choose one or more)."

Tyra says a nice thing about this trick is that the message may go for a couple of days until someone tells the mark. Think of that fun! Then, too, a paranoid mark will blame someone in the office or from home. And, this one can be repeated over and over until the mark catches on.

AUTOMOBILES

It might happen that you need to borrow a car for whatever purpose sometime, and you have only two prerequisites: immediacy and anonymity. Let valet parking come to your need with speed. Here's how.

Find one of those wonderful hotels, motels, resorts, or restaurants that features valet parking. Pick a place too snobbish and proper to issue receipts, which they consider a personal insult. Also, be certain the lot is fairly close to the main area where you'll be.

First, dress appropriately for the environment and the vehicle. Next, go to the lot and select the vehicle you wish to borrow. Note the model, year, color, and plate number. You must then get into the restaurant, motel, or whatever without the car jockies seeing you. Then, you stroll out with confidence and a five- or ten-dollar tip in your fingers and summon your vehicle. You describe your vehicle briskly and even recite the license number if asked. The kid delivers your borrowed car, and you're on your way.

By the way, as an addendum, if you have a nonborrowed car and don't want the license plate to be readable, Dyke Thornbutt told me you can spray WD40 or a similar oil on the vehicle's plates. It will make reading the plate color and numbers difficult to impossible, depending on the lighting and your spraying. Just a good tip from one of our guys on the inside pretending to be one of their guys, a mole in many ways.

◆

Next, we listen to the sage advice of Mike R. from L.A., who knows more nasty tricks than anyone on the Left Coast. Mike had the redass for a rotten little mark who had done some bad things to him. Mike knew that his mark loved his car and planned his vengeance accordingly.

"I peeled a banana and shoved it up into his car's exhaust pipe about two feet with a broom. When the jerk started his car, the banana forced the carbon monoxide fumes back into the fuel system, which literally causes the seal on the transmission to disengage. A mechanic won't find the cause of this trouble very easily."

◆

Rasputin learned the hard way that you just don't trust some people. One of these people stole something personal from Rasputin, so our hearty hero put his shop training from high school to work to pay back his mark, Mr. Buttwipe.

Rasputin found the mark's car, an older

manual-transmission model, cut the brake and accelerator lines, then cross-connected them. Thus, Mr. Buttwipe found he had to press his brake peddle to start his car. Unhappily, he didn't learn this until he had already slammed on his brakes, and instead of stopping, he ran into someone's front porch, knocking it down around his car.

Nothing mad about our monk—Rasputin got even!

◆

The Gooch's mark was an idiot midden named Crapper Kreig who used to park his car in handicapped zones, double-park other cars, and in general be a utility-grade pain in the ass. Happily, Kreig drove a small car. One night, The Gooch and six of his pals picked up the mark's car and placed it lengthwise between two trees.

The Gooch said there was less than six inches clearance front and back so there was no way the mark could drive his car out. He said a two-door car could also be positioned sideways so closely between trees or buildings that the doors could not be opened for the mark to enter the car to drive it away and the car could not be pushed forward or backward without being scratched.

◆

Matt Louis told me that a jerk used to terrorize neighborhood lawns with drunken spins in his 4x4 truck at night. Matt said he waited until a large, icy snowfall was predicted for that special night to pay back the jerk.

"We knew he was at home drunk and wasn't going four-wheeling on our lawns that night. So, a bunch of us got some old logs that had been cut during some lot clearings and stacked them around his vehicle," Matt told me.

Matt says it was like a fort, logs piled on top of each other and locked, like the old Lincoln logs we used to play with as kids. The sleet and icy snow served as the mortar that held the logs together, forming a fortress around the mark's truck, with less than a foot of room between the vehicle and the walls.

"He was shocked, to say the least, the next morning. His truck was surrounded by an icy, frozen wall of logs four feet high," Matt added.

It took nine days for the jerk to get his vehicle loose. He had to buy new tires and a new battery. Why new tires? Well, as an added bonus for this lawn-ripper, Matt and friends poured buckets of water under and around the vehicle's tires, ice-welding them to the turf . . . with more ice and snow to cover.

That mark never again four-wheeled his truck in the neighborhood.

◆

The Magic Z lived near a jerk who used to put-put around late at night in his tiny Hyundai car, dumping his garbage in other people's piles to avoid paying for removal himself.

"It's a tiny little bug of a car. So, one night, six

of us, and we're pretty husky guys, went over to his place. It was late and, for once, all was quiet at his place. We carefully and *very quietly* picked up his Hyundai and gently laid it over on its roof, right in his wife's flower bed. We took half an hour to do it so there'd be no noise, scratches, or dents. It was perfect," Magic reports.

He added that the guy came out the next morning and stood looking at his car for a full ten minutes without moving. His wife came out and started to give him hell. He finally got a crew of people to come from a nearby garage. Using a tow truck and several guys, they eventually got his Hyundai righted, Magic says.

"The best part is that they dented the hood, scratched the finish in three places, and still charged him $125 for the job," Magic added.

◆

My old friend from another life, Carlos Chacal Kopfjaeger, also used a vehicle to get even. Carlos had used the services of a cement contractor who really botched the job, then refused to make it right. My old buddy decided to repay in kind. He picked a cold night when the temperature was expected to drop below zero.

"I took my truck loaded with some old 2 x 10 lumber to this dork's business after hours and, with the help of my cousin, built a set of forms to surround his three trucks. We set plastic inside them, then used his hose to fill the forms with water. Naturally, a lot of water ran out, but enough froze that we eventually had an ice lake eight inches deep and two feet out surrounding each truck. As a real spillover plus, all the approaches to the entire parking area were solid sheets of ice several inches thick."

The dynamic duo went home and got warm, chuckling over whether the cement contractor would get his fleet thawed out enough to work the next day.

◆

Because people eat mostly for fun but also partly for fuel, it is fitting that the Duke of Devious Deeds should come up with an idea that combines both. He wants to help your mark do a bit of baking while the mark and his or her car are running errands or off to work.

"Maybe your mark is going on a picnic or a vacation. Think how much fun and help you could be if you'd set things up so your mark could bake some bread along the way," says Brother Duke.

He suggests adding some flour and yeast to the radiator of your mark's car shortly before departure time. I can see where this would be a real time-saver, because there'd be no loafing around on this short trip. Plus, it sure will get a rise out of the mark.

◆

Hot Rodder views the trend toward higher octane gasoline with ironic humor, noting, "Most people never heard of racing gas. It's really high octane, like 106 or higher. It's also tough to find. But never mind that. Find some and add about five gallons to the fuel tank of your mark's car.

"It will create all sorts of situations, including ruination of the catalytic converter and possibly a blown engine. The engine will also fail emissions tests as there is lead in this racing gas," says Hot Rodder.

◆

Although this is not a car-care tip, Jambo has some advice for those readers who want to have some fun at the expanse of their mark's garage door. He says, "A heavy application of Liquid Nail or PL400 applied all the way around the gaps and seams between the garage door, frame, and jamb will set and seal overnight.

"This can cause anything from morning panic to being late for work and could even screw up an electric garage-door opener."

◆

The Knight says that it's a lot of fun to slip the air filter/cleaner off your mark's auto, then sprinkle a lot of baby powder into the intake fan of the engine. It causes all sorts of nasty dust storms inside the car. I bet you could use any sort of disgusting floating debris: soap powder, sneezing powder, powdered fertilizer, and so on.

BALLOONS

We were sitting around our usual table in the Old Phart Room of Burl Yates' famous Ramit Inn, located just outside the city limits of Grossen Esel, Michigan, discussing bullies. The old Marine, Gunny Steffey, and Doc Hughes were yukking around over memories of youthful fights with older, bigger bullies. Paco Escobar, who once set a deviate priest's hassock on fire, said that the victims of bullies need to come up with a leading edge, an extra punch, a trick to help them win.

We all agreed and spent the next few minutes telling more lies of how we beat back the bullies. Then, Paco came up with his technique. He calls it his Bullybusting Ammonia Balloon Fist.

"It's quite simple to create, even easier to use, and it's effective. This homemade power slammer will make your next encounter with a bully a one-punch winner for you," Paco promises.

He says to force enough ammonia into an ordinary balloon to bulge the rubber pretty well. Paco estimates about two cups will do it. When you're ready for action, you simply smack the mark in the face with the ammonia balloon.

 We were roaring with laughter when a wizened old man at the next next table turned and whined, "Gracious, you chaps are liable to injure someone. Please be careful with your rough talk like that. I'm a sensitive old man." With that, he rose and headed for the door. As he passed our table, Dr. Josef Mengele gave us his business card.

BANKCARDS

Did the Federal Reserve Board really suggest that the government sell advertising space on money? It must be true, since I read it in *USA Today*. I also read in there that you run a 35-percent chance of being ripped off by a money access machine this year. That's a nice thought for your bank, as it cuts their overhead expenses, but what does it do for you? Who cares?

An ATM exceeded its snafu quota twice on The Cheshire Cat last year. Yup, an automatic teller machine ate one of his checks and messed up another of his transactions, all of which cost him time, aggravation, and money. The bank's employees were not sympathetic. They treated him as if he were too dumb to use their machine.

A bright, technically minded guy, The Cheshire Cat has not been declawed and is not someone with whom to mess. Faced with the bank's bad attitude, his response was to zap the machine before it zapped him again. Here is his idea.

His basic tool is a Taser Stun Gun. The rest of his kit includes liquid copper to touch up circuit boards, a tiny brush, a blank plastic bankcard, and a mark that's really been asking for it—in his case that thieving ATM.

"Paint copper on the surface of the blank card to form a grid. Be careful that the line groups not touch each other," Cheshire says. "Do both sides of the card and make sure that the contact points from each side meet at the same points and at the edge of the card."

Next, carefully connect the Taser gun's wires to the points at the edge of the card. You now have a zapper that will bite the bank machine before it bites you or anyone else.

Of course, Cheshire didn't really do this. It's all just fantasy and fun, like everything we do.

◆

Mello Smello's idea doesn't involve bankcards, but the mark is the same. Mr. Smello suggests an entertaining way to amuse yourself by using your checks at the bank's expense, with the added bonus of giving your treasury about three more days to cover said check with long green. Mr. Smello speaks of pricking pinholes between the numbers at the bottom of your check, the area where the machine scans/reads it. The pinholes shut all of that down, causing a real human to have to process the check, according to Mr. Smello.

Don't feel too sorry for the banks that issue bankcards. Remember, Mark Twain told you that banks are like someone who rents you an umbrella when the sun is shining and wants it back the minute the rain starts. Personally, I always thought of a bank official as a pawnbroker with a white shirt, tie, and manicure.

BAR BANDS

I was in a good-old-boys bar in Baton Rouge with my friend, Calhoun Tubbs, as the bar band finished its second set. Calhoun knew the band's leader, so we sat and talked about the fun and games facing bar bands that play the less than honorable markets.

"It's amazing the bullshit you put up with in those tank town dumps," the leader drawled. "The biggest hassle is getting cheated on your cut of the house... it's the most common rip-off, too."

Being the good samaritan that I am, I told this lad about some of the advice I'd heard from Eugene Chadbourne, a talented guitarist/musician, band founder, and very strange chap. One of his basic paybacks—learned from hard years on the road—is flushing a popsicle stick down each commode in a dump owned by someone who's cheated you.

Another of this musical master's scores to settle involves placing calls to various booking agents on behalf of your mark's bar or music club and canceling various upcoming shows. Dr. Chadbourne says that you obviously need the special inside knowledge of the business to work this one effectively.

As anyone who's been near the smell will tell you, showbiz attracts more than its share of putrid pygmies. They must have been discussing one of these when Uncle Chris and his pal Brett, who's with that great doo-wop band, The DeVilles, told me about lyrical switch.

Now, the only game called switch I'd ever heard about had its origins in the military and involved one's thumb, one's mouth, one's anus, and an NCO's command. I suspect that game is gone, along with brown boots, discipline, and real citizen soldiers.

"If you have a mark or two in the bar, perhaps the owner or maybe a least favorite bartender or godzilla weightress, you improvise a verse of nasty nonsense about that mark, or you just improvise some lyrics," they explained.

Ahh, I thought, that's just like when Mick Jagger and other ancients used to substitute obscene lyrics into their songs just to piss off the establishment. The boys agreed, naming today's groups that do the same thing.

"We're just suggesting you can localize it to fit your mark or your situation."

The honor of all this imaginative musical splendor caused me to create some titles soon to be classics on the national playlist, to include, "Tequila Mockingbird," and one I want to dedicate to all the pro-life Nazis, "Fecund to Nun." Perhaps a new heavy metal group called Oedipus Wrecks will perform these at Tipper Gore's inauguration party after the 1998 election.

BOATS

If your mark owns a boat with a trolling motor on it, Biggus Piraphicus has some good news for you. I have friends who troll, but it's for birds, not fish. I also know a couple of trolls who own boats. Sorry, Biggus, I digress . . .

He suggests you do your necessary technical study so that you accomplish this properly. But, once done, it's a real gas, he says. You rewire the foot-pedal control so that it goes to the main motor for the boat, as well as the trolling motor propeller. As Biggus says, your mark will be in for a major, and quite possibly wet, surprise.

◆

Rollo Gumpox once introduced me to a man who was to be his main mark. The beauty of it was that the target never knew of Rollo's revenge. Part of Rollo's humor was introducing me to the mark beforehand.

The guy looked like a mark. He was rude, mean, bigoted, and otherwise quite nasty. His face reminded me of someone's beefy, red, bare buttocks wearing glasses.

This mark owned a boat, and he had knowingly and sneakily cheated Rollo and a lot of other people out of borrowed gasoline, boat care, docking fees, fishing gear, clients, and fish. He was King Mooch.

Rollo chained Mr. Mark's boat, via heavy chain and cable strung under the water, to a rather frail-appearing private mooring and social platform at a bar about fifty feet away. Considering that Mr. Mark always took off with throttles firewalled, well . . . you get the idea.

Rollo reports, "I did this about four weeks after you met him. The bar owner sued him, charging him with deliberately doing the damage. Incidentally, he totally wrecked the place and also messed his own motor. Because everyone hated him, nobody listened to his perfectly logical argument of why would he use his own boat in broad daylight? He settled out of court and moved to another marina. I'm satisfied."

Rollo celebrated in anonymity, of course—the only way.

BOMBS

Stink bombs have been a favorite "gotcha" for many people in many poses for long periods of time. The Magic Z is acquainted with a stink bomb that will, in his words, "melt the doors off Ft. Knox." Having spent my basic training time there, I'm impressed with that power.

To create this maximum nauseater, mix powdered hydrogen sulfide with vinegar and let it dry to a paste. Next, *very carefully* remove some of the gunpowder from an M80, M60, or homemade firecracker. Replace some of the powder with the dried paste. Magic Z says fifty/fifty is a nice ratio.

When detonated, the loud explosion is followed by a major cloud of awful smoke that would bring major tears to a noseless corpse. Indeed, it is probably worse than the odor of a death fart, if you've ever smelled one of those bombs. I might match Uncle Gerald's deadly dew against it, though.

Mr. Magic says to experiment to get the proper mixture of sulfide to vinegar. But, *be careful!*

◆

J.J. of Boston introduced me to one of the cheapest of smelly bombs, a common potato. He says to take a large potato, bang it and bruise it around a bit, then hide it somewhere in your mark's environment, e.g., a desk drawer, a file cabinet, under a bed, in a storage box.

Give a potato four or five weeks, especially a large, bruised one, and it will smell very, very much and very awful. J.J. adds that you can use more than one potato if you want to cause more talk about the mark, and/or his office, home, or whatever.

The potato is a cheap and highly disgusting stench bomb. If the media prissies get hold of that information, they'll start their usual biased bullying of Congress to pass potato-control laws.

BUGS

To begin with, these are the James Bond-type of bugs, not the insect type. Although this stunt is a tad expensive, it can also be great fun. Of course, the expense involved is in buying the bugging equipment. But, as Calhoun Tubbs points out, there are many grants-in-aid available to obtain this sort of equipment inexpensively. He refers to the Back-of-the-Truck-Mart, Ye Olde Five Finger Discount, and so forth.

Among the advocates of this sort of fun are Storm Trooper, Charlene D., and Reggie Yorke. Their application is fairly generic.

Charlene, a gorgeous woman with a wonderfully fun imagination, says, "What you need are a transmitting radio and a very small, wireless receiver/speaker. The idea is to covertly plant the receiver/speaker somewhere very inopportune for your mark, then do your transmitting over that speaker."

Applications include hiding such a unit in a fast-food restaurant that has offended you. That way you can "help out" by broadcasting additional or confusing orders. Or, you can add extra conversation or offer social, ethnic, or racial comments sure to offend some of its customers.

"The point is that it might take the management awhile to find your speaker, especially if you've stashed several," Charlene adds. "In one case, it was fun to plant them in the restrooms and comment on the physical characteristics of various patrons. You'd be surprised how many people get insulted and don't tell the management. Think about it."

She said you can also plant a small speaker actually on the mark's person and have "them" say inappropriate things to others via your voice.

◆

Laughing, Bluetooth Kneesupper recalled a similar situation where he'd planted a bug in the stall of a woman's restroom and monitored the patrons entering the facility from his car.

"One very large lady went in, and I waited for enough time to elapse for her to get fully into operation, then I shouted into the transmitter, 'Ohhh, ouuch, geez, lady, move your lard ass. You're smashing me. I can't breathe. Damn you, you tonnablubber, get your fat ass off my head.' Sure enough, about thirty seconds later, here comes this enormous bison of a woman steaming out of the door and straight to the manager's office."

Bluetooth says he stayed quiet while the

manager searched the room. He didn't find the bug, and Bluetooth used it again that day, and again, and again.

◆

Getting back to real bugs, of the crawly insect kind, Zero Man claims that termites are a far better assault on a building than stink bombs or noxious chemicals. He says to dump bags of termites into your mark's buildings.

"It's good revenge, as the damage doesn't show up right away. And, these little helpers are so easy to collect. Try a nearby sawmill that has very old sawdust. They'll be there," he promises.

BULLIES

Here's a jerk out of everyman's childhood, the neighborhood or schoolyard bully. You usually spot them lumbering around with their knuckles dragging on the ground. Terrible Tom knew one of these subhuman species from his days of working in a store in which youngsters hung out.

"He'd come in and start picking on the quiet kids, the ones he knew were afraid to fight back," Tom said. "This continued into college. By then, he'd graduated into a second-string football player, which is how he got into college in the first place, and first-team bully. A major in physical education, a haven for numb-minded jocks, he was happy when starting fights, date raping, drunk/puking, shit like that."

Tom got his inspiration one day when this troglodyte came into his rooming house, the only thing they shared, bragging about how tough he was, i.e., how he'd just bested a karate student in a brawl. Tom added, "Never mind that the kid was sixteen years old and gave up one-hundred pounds and a lot of fear to this giant."

Tom knew that even a 2 x 4 would break over this cretin's skull, so he used his own skull and some desktop publishing equipment available at the school.

"I printed some handbills that I placed in every karate school and tough-guy bar in the area. The handbill read, 'You've Messed with the Rest, Now Lose to the Best,' and went on to explain how tough the mark was. Mr. Bully, a.k.a. the mark, had his name and address at the bottom of the flyer," Tom said.

Terrible Tom added that within the next ten days, Mr. Bully became Mr. Meek. He also sported a black eye and several nasty bruises and cuts on his face, and he spent a few days in the local hospital during that period.

As Terrible Tom explained, it's truly amazing how an attitude adjustment is possible, even from a big, bad bully. I agree.

◆

Or, consider a gentle friend of mine from some years past, the kind of guy you know is going to be bullybait—soft, fey, pale, and studious. I asked him about bullies once.

"Oh, yeah, George, I do attract them, usually when I'm with a date or in a bar alone," Harry told me. "I've learned that you never back down or away. If you do, you'll always lose. So, I've learned each time just to kick that bully in the balls so hard that he'll have pubic hair caught in his throat for a week."

I was really impressed, especially when he

explained his follow-through, "I usually kick 'em twice, topple them, then stomp on some ribs hard enough to break 'em. Finally, I carry a licensed .45 and show it to the bully at that point. It's usually quite enough."

What are my friends becoming? First, it was Rosey Grier doing needlepoint, then Bob Brown with this flowered underwear, and now Harry with his kicks and .45 pistol.

BUMPER STICKERS

Bumper stickers are to yahoos what philosophy is to an educated society. Personally, I love a society that can create its own philosophy in a bumper sticker. Can't you just hear the late H.L. Mencken down there watching someone's car pull out of a K-Mart parking lot with a BOOB ON BORED sticker?

The Toledo Pilot, an aviator, not a newspaper, thank God, gets upset with some of the grosser bumper sticker messages, however. Hardly a prude, this veteran flier would rather not have someone else's crude values forced on him in traffic. He told me about a little stunt he uses.

"I know an obnoxious guy who has an equally obnoxious bumper sticker that reads 'SHIT HAPPENS.' One night I added another sticker to his car bumper, right next to the old one. The new one read, 'IT SURE DOES, AND I'M LIVING PROOF.'"

He said he had a supply of similar signs printed, so he can strike again and again. Observe, you White Ribbon Assholes, he's not trying to censor somebody else's views, he's commenting on and adding to them. That's good First Amendment democracy.

◆

My graphic friend GI—no, not that sort of GI (shudder)—printed a bumper sticker for his own truck. It reads, "I BRAKE FOR TAILGATERS."

CABLE TELEVISION

Happy day to you, it's another technological tomahawk to bury in your mark's thick, deserving skull, all courtesy of Warhawk. He likes the computerized, artificial intelligence world in which we live because it gives him new ways to get back at deserving bullies. In his case, he knew a man who used to ruin an entire neighborhood's TV reception by using his ham radio equipment and power tools. No amount of pleading for some neighborly understanding helped. The jerk was a boor.

In Warhawk's market area, you can use your Touch Tone telephone to obtain pay-per-view cable service. Naturally, Warhawk used a pay phone for his caper. First, he dialed the cable system's phone number and followed the instructions given by the automated voice. Warhawk then dialed in his mark's phone number. The voice will confirm what you've just ordered.

Warhawk says, "You have now purchased for your mark a TV event that will be billed to his telephone number. The cost ranges from four to thirty-five dollars, depending upon the event. The funniest part is that the mark doesn't realize what has happened until the bill arrives, creating even more blood-pressure-enhancing fun."

Not only is the program selection unlimited, so are the directions from which you can come at this one. The Gonnif Cable Company in Gungrabber, New Jersey, messed up billing for its customers and was both nasty and slow about correcting its errors.

The owner of this system was one of those fast-talking sleaze merchants who could turn Mother Teresa into a mall abortionist. But, as his was the only system in town, there was no relief—until a certain avenger, Ronin, got involved.

Since he couldn't physically fire off a can of Mace up the owner's ass, Ronin decided to use national, state, and local government regulatory agencies as a substitute suppository. Here is just a teaser list of some of his early stunts. As this is an active campaign, I will be brief and somewhat generic.

- Phony bills on fake invoices went to noncustomers, including some government biggies.
- Using fairly sophisticated technology, Ronin was able to "give" certain customers adult entertainment channels, substituting them for religious ones. Customers included both institutional and individual members of right-wing, fanatical religions.

- Using telephone technology, he discontinued service to selected customers, followed by a letter the next day dunning them for chronic nonpayment.
- Late night calls heckled, hectored, and hassled would-be customers to subscribe to the service.

As that legendary old blues king, Watery Bowels, once told me about another nasty who got hit, "Hee, hee, hee, that fucker be in for a planet-sized ass-chewing from a whole lotta nasty peoples."

Ahmen, Watery. It sure fits here, too.

CAR DEALERS

Peter Upitis is not the sort of man you'd suspect of having such a devastating response to an unscrupulous car dealer who tried to scam him into buying. You're about to read why he is just that sort of man.

First, here's the premise. The unsuspecting customer drives his or her car to the dealership. The salesthing greets the customer and finally convinces him or her that a test drive is in order.

While the customer is off on the drive, one of the dealer's minions has that customer's car towed to a nearby storage garage. The salesthing and customer return and can't find the customer's car.

Several minions and the sales manager confer, then the "horrified" manager comes to the customer and admits to a major mistake.

"I am so sorry. I thought we'd just bought your car, and, now, I'm afraid it's already on its way to the auto auction in Scumville (a distant city). It will take us two days to get it back," the manager whimpers.

Then, the manager and salesthing blurt out, almost in chorus, "But, here's what we'll do. While we send someone to get your car, you take this new car you just drove. Take it home, free, no charge or anything. Use it, let your family use it. It's on us, and you have our apologies. We'll get your old car back and clean it up for you. Geez, we're really sorry."

The scam, according to Peter, is that the customer takes the new car home for the weekend or two days or whatever, and everyone in the family and neighborhood loves it so much that when it's time to trade back to the old car, the customer has fallen in love with the new one and a deal is made . . . with "a big discount to make up for the inconvenience." Peter says it's all a deliberate act.

I was aghast when I heard this. To verify this dastardly duplicity, I called Gerald Delmonte, a former auto dealership magnate who now operates a personal-care home in Sanibel, Florida, for golden-years bimbos. An old compatriot of mine, he'd be honest, I knew.

"Oh yes, it's a common enough trick of weak, crooked salespeople. I know dealers who still use that old con," Gerald told me. He also wanted to know if Peter had suggested a remedy.

Peter Upitis had two cures for this diseased thinking. First, take the new car out that night and enter it in a demolition derby. It's not your car, you know. And, you might get lucky and win some money.

Or, when you come back and find the scam pulled and your old car gone, slip into your acting mode and, with a catch in your voice, say, "Oh, my God, my year-old son was asleep in the backseat. He has a severe infection and needs his medicine in the next half hour. Oh my God, I'd better call 911."

It's amazing how quickly the dealer will have someone "intercept" and return your old car to you. You run to the car, peer in the backseat, and scream, "My son's been kidnapped!" Then, you jump in your car and shout that you're going to the police and then to your lawyer.

You never return.

Gerald added that you could also try out the new car as an off-road vehicle, enter it in a hill climb, or do a home video of one of those commercials where a car climbs a pile of cement blocks.

As consumers, it's nice to know that we have allies like Peter Upitis and Gerald Delmonte.

◆

Gibson Hoople was a kindly sort who bought the same make of car each time—a regular, solid customer until an import manufacturer decided to ignore him when he complained after four or five unsuccessful attempts to repair major problems with his new car. Although his state had a lemon law, the manufacturer ignored Gibson and his requests. They put him on permanent hold.

Many car makers carry the infection of greed like Mary Mallon carried typhoid. This car maker had not planned on our pal Gibson's imagination and dedicated fury. Unlike his surname, he was no hoople.

Gibson was creative and intuitive. He could smell the farts of this fraudulence before they even sat down to their suitmen lunches. He knew they couldn't take the heat of the kitchen.

What he did was take photos of his own car, using Japanese film, of course, to produce composite layouts. He used logos and advertising claims from the car maker's own brochures, which he picked up from another dealership, and a live lemon from a nearby market.

He made large paste-up originals of very specific auto "ads," then reshot them on another roll of film, producing postcard-sized photos of several satiric messages. Each was about as subtle as wiping one's ass with a chain saw.

He next got the names of people who worked in both management and clerical positions at the car maker's New Jersey offices and began sending them "holiday" postal cards during his business trips. He also distributed copies of the lemon-car-ad photos, made cheaply by a local printer, to his friends for them to send to employees of the car maker and dealers in their areas.

You have to see the cards to get true enjoyment from Gibson Hoople's little payback. Indeed, if you'd like one, I have a few of the postcards he gave me, and they are free for as long as the supply lasts.

CB RADIOS

It's grand old Ray Heffer again, Kansas City's kindly commando of fun and games, with some advice on using your CB radio to pay back evil bullies. You still do have a CB radio, don't you, good buddy?

Get a linear amplifier for your CB radio, even though it is illegal to hook one up to a CB, according to federal, as in Federal Communications Commission (FCC), regulation and all of that nonsense. This sort of unit is designed to amplify two-way radio signals far beyond their normal output. For example, maximum power on a CB is four watts. Some linear amps run as high as four hundred watts.

They are illegal, but as old George knows, a dime can cover the moon if you hold it in front of your eyes properly. Try hobby swap meets, truck stops, flea markets, or radio phreaks as sources.

Here's one of Heff's CB tricks. Some new automobiles have computerized fuel-metering systems, including Ford Taurus, some of the sportier VW models, and Mercury Sable. Drive close to your mark's vehicle with your CB on and your linear amplifier hooked up and on. Key your mike.

The enormous and excessive RF energy from the souped-up CB will oversaturate the vehicle's fuel-metering computer and stall the engine. Be careful, though, that you don't cause a major accident.

◆

Reading newspaper stories about truck-stop dollies, Yeb Vas and his friend Betty Nargilah came up with a fun way to pay back this overpainted trixie from Betty's office who was seducing married men, then calling their wives to report the affair, pretending to be Betty.

They dug out their old CB, hooked it up, and went out on a hilltop near a popular truck stop. There, in her sexiest low voice, Betty pitched herself as the Highway Hooker. Using short transmissions at random times, she advertised herself as the finest, warmest, and best lay-lady in five states. The kicker was that she gave out the office trixie's phone number as the number to call to make an appointment.

After two nights of this, when Betty went to work the third day, there was a small vase on her desk and in it were a single white rose and a small white flag.

No more problems in that office.

CIA

This stunt will work with the unwitting cooperation of any government spookery, including the KGB, FBI, NSA, DIA, DEA, MADD, et. al. Hell, intelligence agencies are more intertangled than the bodies at a San Francisco orgy. I chose the CIA for this heading simply because I can spell it. The idea involves cryptogram coding and comes to us from long-time friend Chris Schaefer.

Chris says to send a letter in the form of a serious cryptogram to some fictional person in the USSR, Libya, China, Cambodia, Iraq, North Korea, or some other bastion of freedom (hey, that could include the old U.S. of A!). The letter needs to be addressed to that fictional person at "General Delivery" in some city in that country.

Make sure that you include your mark's name and home address as the sender of this mysterious missive. As you know, the intelligence services of all dictatorships and police states, including our own, intercept and read letters. If you want to ensure that yours is intercepted, send it to a fictional character or title at some military or spy institution.

What's a cryptogram? It's a message that has been encoded in some way. A simple form of code involves writing your sentences in vertical columns without punctuation so as to get five or six columns. For example, consider:

```
H  K  S  D
A  I  G  F
Y  N  R  U
D  G  A  N
U  I  N
```

To the ordinary mortal it looks like a doctor's eye chart, but to the sorcerers in the kingdom of spookery it is obviously a crypto code. What did I write in my example? Spread it out in more conventional, horizontal format and you get HAYDUKING IS GRAND FUN. Of course, you don't send that silly message. Use a message involving assassination, bombs, drugs, or some other topic sure to quicken the pulse of a paranoid intelligence officer.

Chris says you might want to send a whole series of letters. That way it looks conspiratorial and real. It will mean lots of fun for your mark. Read your spy novels so you can get good pithy messages.

FBI, CIA, DIA, DNA, MI5, NSA, KGB, ONI . . . what's in a name? They're all fingers of the same dirty glove.

COMPUTERS

Orotund Vowel had a very pious gal pal who hated most everything sexual. In less gender-sensitive days, we would have called Orotund's femme friend a humorless, frigid prude. On several social occasions, she had caused embarrassment by objecting to any small talk that even hinted at sexual content, then made a point of hectoring Orotund's friends for even thinking about sex.

Orotund had heard of SeXXY Software, a small outfit in Pennsylvania that specializes in adult computer entertainment (see Sources). He got their SeXXY Disk #1, which opens with a graphic color photo of a woman's face. It's not a cartoon, but an actual graphic, as close as you can get to a photo on a computer screen.

Orotund loaded a copy disk of SeXXY #1 onto his gal pal's computer, and the photo appeared, a lovely portrait of a lovely lady. Now, then, the fun. When any key is punched on the computer, the program runs. The very next scene is that same woman with a very large penis in her mouth. At this point, the screen becomes active as the lady does a very graphic fellatio number in full living, moving, action color right to the tasteful climax.

Orotund says his former lady friend had several of her like-minded sisters at her place when she discovered the innocent portrait on her computer screen. He told me that she failed to share the humor and that he was no longer welcome in her life. He said he was very appreciative for small favors and big laughs.

This exact stunt was practiced by Max Output on his stuffy, workaholic, total-hassle-causing department head who was scheduled for an early morning conference. For her presentation, the department head planned to use a management program she thought was loaded on the computer.

The suitfolk gathered and she hit the computer's start key. You know what was to cum on the screen. You read it here first. According to Max, many of the office pee-ons saw the show through her large on-floor window before she could get to the machine to shut it off.

Another amusing software program is called Pranks and is the work of Dale McKinnon, president of The Modern Advisory Institute (see Sources). His Pranks is a collection of somewhat harmless practical jokes that can be inserted on or into your mark's computer system.

One of the programs, Crumble, got a great deal of notoriety for surreptitiously finding its way into any manner of corporate product demonstrations, sales programs and institutional systems. For example, in 1988, someone mysteriously introduced Crumble into a computer demonstration at a Lotus Corporation marketing meeting, at which the company's salespeople were showing off Lotus 1-2-3. Naturally, the Lotus suitmen were horrified at this gentle humor. Another of the programs in Pranks is called Insults and is a delight to set up on your mark's computer or on behalf of your mark on someone else's computer.

◆

Tyra Pierce has updated and upgraded some of his computer Haydukery from several books ago. As he notes, times and computers have changed since our early days of innocence. Now it seems everyone has a hard drive along with a floppy. Often people trust these hard drives enough not to back up their files, thinking their data will never be lost. Listed below are the DOS commands for completely reformatting a hard drive and wiping everything clean. Recovering the data is an extremely expensive undertaking.

First, it's important to get into DOS or into the system. If the screen has a symbol like C>, that means you're in DOS. If you're using a menu-selection program, look carefully at the screen and find the command to exit the program. When you find that, exit the program and enter the following commands.
CD..
CD..
FORMAT C: /S

At this point, the program will either proceed or give a message reading, "BAD COMMAND OR FILE NAME." If this happens, enter CD DOS. If this command doesn't work, and you don't have a knowledge of computers, just abort—but the thought was there! If things go well, the next line should state:

"WARNING, ALL DATA ON NONREMOVABLE DISK DRIVE C: WILL BE LOST! PROCEED WITH FORMAT? (Y/N)"

The appropriate answer is Y.

You will then hear the disk reformatting itself. If you have some time and want to be cocky, you can leave your mark a message that will appear whenever he or she next turns on the machine. After the machine is through ridding itself of your mark's valuable data, type in the following:

COPY CON AUTOEXEC.BAT
C> Type your message here.
Press the control key and Z at the same time.
Press enter.

Shut off the computer. When the mark powers up the next time, he or she will find a nice clean hard drive, and after the computer people finish recovering the data, the mark's wallet will be as clean as the drive had been.

CREDIT

Creditors are the people who show up because the customer's money didn't. The people who often collect for these creditors usually are built like refrigerators with eyes. As I've noted in past books there are many amusing ways to use credit to your advantage while disadvantaging your mark. One specific vignette comes from Mahng Tia, who explains how you get private information about your mark in a later section of this same book (see In Privity).

Unless your mark is rich, when he or she needs to make a major purchase, it's borrow-money time, just like the rest of us, from some chinless wonder at a financial institution. Good grief, I just caught myself almost being maudlin about a mark's commonality. Sorry, that won't happen again.

Perhaps you don't want your mark to be able to borrow money. Isn't it fun to have that sort of power? You do have it, you know . . . well, sort of, anyway. According to Mahng Tia, here's what to do. Obtain a number of those ubiquitous credit applications that seem to grow on the counters of stores, shops, and restaurants everywhere. Collect some of the mail-order ones and some from the lesser financial institutions.

You'll include the legitimate personal information about your mark (that you learned to gather in the section on In Privity). However, where the form asks for place of employment, get creative and write down "Self-Employed." List income at about $30,000. My credit-bureau sources tell me that the word "Self-Employed" stands out like a politician at a saints convention. List as many credit cards as you wish for your mark. Where it asks for both the home and business telephone numbers, list the home phone for both.

Mail one or two completed cards every ten days or so. All of this activity, especially with that red flag of self-employment, will put your mark in the credit-denied category for anywhere from one to four months in most states. By the time the company checks things out and/or the mark gets wise, you can start all over again. My in-house experts tell me that few companies have enough skilled investigators to do a real check on this situation, so you might deny credit to your mark for a long, long time.

OK, gang, now that we've all had a good laugh over this, you have to promise me that you won't ever really *do* anything like this to anyone. As the wonderfully funny Richard Pryor might say, "Whoooa, this is some serious shit." But, it's damned funny, too.

CREDIT CARDS

Fletcher Dristui used to be a bouncer for the Chuck E. Cheese restaurant group before he opened his shops. He also was a credit-card company executive for ten years. He told me about how a friend of his, a chap named Bubba, got unjustly fired by another fast-food outfit and how Bubba got back.

"This place took credit cards. Now, what you need to know is that all card companies have 800 numbers for store employees to call in credit-card-authorization checks. Each store also has its own identification number. Also, all card companies publish bad card lists," Fletcher said. "You put all of that together and you can have some fun with your store/mark."

If you want to have some fun with a sleazy shop or restaurant, make a record of the card company's 800 number(s), also the mark/store's card ID number, then get a bunch of credit-card numbers from that list of bad cards. Try to get numbers of cards that have been recalled or marked as unauthorized and of cards issued by a local bank, if you can. Why? Keep reading.

Next, Fletcher says to call the 800 number, identify yourself as the manager of the shop, give that ID number, then ask to verify a specific card, number such and such. Of course, you pick one of the awful cards from the hit list.

Do this during banking hours because the card company will call the local issuing bank, and in a few moments, a bank officer will show up at the shop to collect the errant card. Fletcher says that bankers sometimes bring a cop along to arrest the cardholder if fraud is suspected.

Straightening this out will be fun, fun, fun . . .

As Roberta and Genifer once told me, "Money isn't everything, but it comes in handy when you've forgotten your credit cards."

DEADBEATS

Never borrow serious money from a friend. As Rabelais wrote, the loan of a small amount will create a debtor; the loan of a large amount can create an enemy. Dastardly Dan made a pragmatist out of that ancient philosopher when a "friend" stiffed him for a "fair amount of money I couldn't afford to lose," as he explained.

He had loaned his pal the money and was given a check to repay the loan. The check stretched further than his pal's credit or credibility, i.e., it bounced. Twice more, Dan went through the bad-check routine. He finally asked his pal for a cash repayment. His friend was never home and never returned phone calls.

"At this point, I decided to turn this matter over to another approach. I did have one of his blank checks, which I'd gotten during one of my visits to his home. I'd grabbed it while his wife was distracted," Dan explained.

"I took that blank check and an ad from a Sunday newspaper that offered twenty-five personalized checks for five dollars. I sent off a money order and ordered the new checks 'for my pal.' Only I filed an address change . . . to a post-office box I opened in his name.

"When the checks arrived I was all ready, with twenty-five different orders to twenty-five different mail-order companies and local businesses. Much of what I ordered was fairly big-ticket items, too."

Dan said he carefully mailed the letters, avoiding fingerprints, then walked away from his ex-pal's life. Dan adds, "I never went near that rented post-office box, and I never again called that swine. I had already written off my money to him as a 'lost loan' on my income tax that year."

Dan reports that he heard nothing more about the matter, but a friend at the bank told him that he'd heard the ex-pal was in hot water with a bunch of companies, the bank, and the post office.

DOCTORS

Since I'm a rural rustic and my doctor is an old-fashioned kind of neat guy who works out of a small clinic in an equally small settlement, I don't have any of the usual doctoral problems that seem to fall upon so many other folks. My doctor is prompt and honest, and he goes about his business fairly, professionally, inexpensively, and with common sense. After talking with other folks about their medical experiences, I consider myself very fortunate.

Unhappily, Storm Trooper's experiences with the men of medicine have been malodorous. He tells me that recently a nurse ended his half-hour wait in a room full of magazines and other patients by ushering him into an examining room. It was small and had no magazines. "Doctor will be with you shortly," Storm Trooper was told.

After twenty minutes of no doctor, no sound, and no magazines, our healthy hero got bored and began to remove the inspection stickers from all of the medical equipment in the room. They were considerable.

"I found out later that I had to wait while 'Doctor' spoke with his golfing partner of the day before. I have a job, too, and my time's worth something to me," Storm Trooper fumed.

A day or so later, Storm Trooper had a friend with a bureaucratic voice call the doctor, identify himself as being with the state medical certification board, and mention that there'd been a complaint about this doctor using uninspected equipment. According to the caller, the bottom line was: the consumer was talking lawsuit.

The flabbergasted doc ran to his room and discovered the lack of inspection stickers. He came back on the line and expressed his astonishment. Storm Trooper's friend said that an inspector would be along that afternoon to get his statement and that he should have his attorney present, as absence of these stickers was very serious.

Storm Trooper wondered how long the doctor and his attorney waited and how many state bureaucrats they had to speak with to straighten out the mess. He had occasion to visit this doctor again three months later and saw that new stickers were in place. As his visit was prompt and agreeable, he saw no reason to reteach the lesson.

DOPE

Ahahahaha, you thought this section was about Ronald Reagan or little Danforth. Nahh, it's about a wonderful idea by Piper Pub to help your mark's foreign vacation or business trip escape the boring blahs with some unexpected excitement.

As Piper points out, most nations today are death on drugs, even harmless ones like marijuana. This politically motivated campaign of hysteria keeps the good citizens from such mundane thoughts as unemployment, homelessness, and hunger. Naturally, your mark would never take drugs in any event, personally or elsewhere. That's where you enter the game.

Your mark is going to one of those death-to-drugs countries, and you're going to make him a happy-dust hero. To celebrate, you buy your mark a new set of moderately priced luggage or a new, large, top-quality suitcase. You have it/them delivered a day or so before the trip along with a printed explanation that the luggage is a prize the mark has won from . . . here you name the mark's favorite radio or TV station, magazine sweepstakes, or something like that. Make your story plausible, yet not easily verified in a short period of time.

However, before you have the luggage delivered, you follow Piper's suggestion and prepare a couple of clever hiding places in the luggage. Consult the book *How to Hide Anything* by Michael Connor (available from Paladin Press) for suggestions. Naturally, you hide some sort of illegal, mind-altering, organic substance or chemical in these locations.

Confirm your mark's departure and arrival with the airline. Give your mark a few hours to unpack and relax in that death-to-drugs nation. Then, as a good citizen, make that international telephone call to their police. Don't call ours, call theirs. Also, use a pay phone and not one in your town unless you live in a very large city. That's a nasty stunt, Piper. Thank you.

Don't try that one at home, kids. It's not as much fun as in a foreign country.

◆

Speaking of drugs, my old pal and fellow trickster Tommie Titmouse passes along an idea with the potential kick of a mule. Tommie points out that our beloved U.S. Supreme Court has ruled that we, the people, have no personal rights at all when coming through customs. They can strip search you, X-ray you, or keep you in detention until you take a dump in your drawers, all in the name of this asinine and murderous political scam that your president calls his war on drugs. That's right, you have none, and they also can do it to your ninety-year-old grandmother.

Customs has an 800 number for squealers to report their fellow citizens for doing things. As I write this, the number is 1-800-BE ALERT, but it's probably changed so check for the new number.

What if your mark is spending time in Canada, Mexico, France, or wherever, and you don't feel like buying new luggage to load for him or her? Brother Titmouse says to give that 800 number a call. You can supply the rest.

◆

According to the DEA, kissing toads won't bring you a prince or princess, and it won't give you warts. It might make you high, though. According to a DEA advisory issued in August 1990, the Cane toad, a large specimen found in the southern U.S., produces a substance known as bufotenine to ward off predators. Chemists say that this substance—taken raw or cooked—will make a human high . . . it's a hallucinogen.

This substance is also found in tropical mushrooms, and my scholarly friends tell me they've used it for years in religious ceremonies, i.e., to get high.

According to a DEA official with whom I spoke, bufotenine is a controlled substance, but that the toads are not illegal to own. I presume you could not lick your toad on purpose, otherwise . . . We may be onto something here. Perhaps we need toad control about like we need more gun control. Let's put that bossy old never-was Ann Landers on this.

◆

There is this wonderful story about Boswell and Johnson being out in the streets of nether London. Johnson would give all of his spare change to street kids, and on their way home, Boswell asked him why he did that, complaining that the kids would only spend the money on booze.

Johnson replied, "Pray, why deny them the only bit of pleasure in their lives?"

I wonder, if our asshole politicians could ever look beyond their re-election posturing, if they might see this is the same situation in our inner cities today?

FIRE

Yup, you thought this section would deal exclusively with arson, and you were about to inform the anti-Hayduke Division of the Department of Just Us. Wrong. It's just another helpful household hint from sweet Dick Smegma.

We start off like one of those Andy Rooney deals. You know, didja ever wonder what would happen if you replaced the easily shattered glass in one of those *Break Glass in Case of Fire* cabinets with either unbreakable Plexiglas or bullet-proof armored glass?

It's just a thought, which got me thinking that you might want to tip off the fire department and/or your mark's insurance company about this amazing finding. Could it be that your mark was about to set an insurance fire and that you, an anonymous whistle blower, saved the day? Why else would that evil, plotting mark do such a dangerous thing as to replace the original and breakable glass, unless . . . Oh, never mind, you could add, it's probably silly to think that way.

That, dear friends, is the sound of the seed of

mistrust being planted. It will sprout into a weed that will bear bitter fruit for your mark. And Shadow knows that for a fact.

◆

Smegma has another way of firing back at retardants who make his life miserable—or, in this case, miserable for a friend of his. It seems an insensitive boor had dropped ashes and drinks on the friend's carpet with no apology or no clean-up, just continued repetition of the same.

"The timing was so fine," Smegma relates. "The boor was in my friend's home doing nasty, sloppy mess/stuff, while an accomplice of my friend was on a mission of mercy to the boor's place."

It seems the accomplice inserted the nozzle of an industrial-sized fire extinguisher into the mail slot of the front door of the boor's place and activated the device, spreading foam all through the foyer and living room. Word was it took five hours of a professional cleaner's time to get rid of the mess, plus one carpet had to be replaced.

FISH

My friend Howard Packer once described a three-day dead fish as the only thing that could smell worse than one of Bruno McManmon's next-day beer farts. I thought that fairly useful until The Stinger, a crewman on a California half-day fishing boat, told me about a fish called sculpin.

It's a nasty, ugly, little bottom dweller, about three pounds of nasty disposition. It carries a high, spiny dorsal fin loaded with a toxic substance that can cause extreme pain, nausea, and even shock in humans. There is no remedy except time, according to The Stinger.

He emphasizes that the toxin is present in the spines even after they've been carefully removed from the fish and dried. He adds that there are probably hundreds of uses for these spines. I would say so, and I would add that this is one fish story I believe.

◆

If spinal tap isn't your goal, but you wish to gall someone by trashing their fish gaol, Mello Smello, another California chap, says that hydrogen peroxide will float the fish in any aquarium. He suggests that you be generous in your application of this useful liquid.

Other than the fact that they have scales, I have nothing personal against fish. You can stay out of their neighborhood, and they won't move to yours. Usually you don't have to look them in more than one eye at a time, and even that's not mandatory. And, this is one plus they have over many humans—they don't talk, so you can't get trapped into listening to boring human stories.

FOOD

Considering that popcorn is such a popular snack, I am not surprised that many people suggested new ways—other than ingestion—to use this early American vital foodstuff. Thus, I thank Howie Metsandbomb, Mello Smello, Lardbrain, Chignon Barb, and Yummy Aunt Nancy.

Good grief, I used to work for a Mr. Lardbrain some years ago, I really did, which causes me to wonder if a mutant strain of genes might have... Nah, humans and nonhumans can't begat offspring. On the other hand, how'd we get all of those football players at old Jock U these past years? I digress... popcorn!

According to my friends, popcorn is very useful. Some specific suggestions for inclusion of the raw, unpopped varieties include:

- In the kitchen you can hide it in toasters, coffee makers, microwaves, ovens, dishwashers with heat dry, or even charcoal grills.
- You can also add popcorn to foodstuffs, such as mixing in some kernels with hamburger patties, pushing some into frankfurters to be

cooked, or adding to scrambled eggs.
- Wildly popping corn will sound hilarious in your mark's clothes dryer. You can also tape or glue some to a seventy-five-watt or larger light bulb.

If you come up with other or wiser uses for popcorn, please let me know. I'd love to hear or read your hull story.

FORMULAE

As promised last time, here are some fun formulae from Jeff Lube and his pal Doc Byte. These are offered solely for your perusal and information and may also be available in other, more serious books than my meager attempts at humor.

GREEK FIRE

This is neat stuff. I recall reading about its use during our Civil War. It is probably more exciting and perhaps even more dangerous than Greek soap, eh sailor? Here is the formula.

1 part live sulfur
2 parts charcoal of willow
6 parts potassium nitrate

Grind each element into a fine powder and mix. Pour this mixture into a container with a wick or fuse. Light and toss. It will carry the flame wherever it strikes. Hmmm, sort of like the oat bran of napalm?

GENERIC PLASTIC EXPLOSIVE
A four-inch square of styrofoam
1/2 part oil
1 part gasoline

Melt the styrofoam, being careful not to let it get too hot or near a flame. Let it cool to a thick viscosity. Then, mix the three ingredients together in this order: styrofoam, oil, gasoline. Mix in a deep pot and, for God's sake, keep this mixture away from any spark or flame. *Use caution.* Let the mixture cool to 75 to 80 degrees, then mold or form it into any shape you want. It will detonate from a fuze or electrical activator.

Please be warned. This stuff is serious shit. When I was a guest of Uncle Sam's khaki warriors, we taught some people how to make this stuff for serious purposes. They used to lard nuts and bolts in the mixture for the purpose of ventilating and meat-tenderizing any bad guys who happened to be in the proximity of the KAAABOOOM.

NITROGEN TRI-IODINE

According to Carnage, this stuff is real fun and dangerous only if you get carried away with volume or use. Sounds fair enough to me. Here is Carnage's formula for this amusing explosive.

1) Combine 1 part of pure solid iodine crystals with 20 cubic centimeters of concentrated ammonium hydroxide. *Perform this operation very slowly and carefully.*

2) Allow a brownish-red precipitate to form, filter it through paper, and wash with alcohol,

then water. Let it dry.

Carnage notes to use *extreme caution*. "This stuff is very sensitive and very unstable. You place it on Q-tips after it crystallizes. The idea is to toss the Q-tip behind a moving car or person. You get a semimajor explosion," says Carnage.

I guess if you tossed a bunch of these into the midst of a bunch of rag-head terrorists, you could write a story called "Farewell to Alms."

FUNERALS

It's arguable which holds the largest measure of self-deception: religion, law enforcement, or education. Biggus Piraphicus would probably vote one-third shares to each. Nonetheless, Biggus told me one of the most bizarre stories of payback for a money-grubbing televangelist I've ever heard.

When Rev. Jerkwad Crooks wasn't skimming money from his naive, faithful followers, he enjoyed bullying clients at abortion-counseling centers, signing gun-grabber petitions, and encouraging the slope-browed goons from his telecongregation to firebomb stores that sold *Playboy* and other magazines he claimed were created to tear down the Republic.

Thus, Biggus felt fortunate when he was able to convince this holy man to do the funeral of Biggus' "departed aunt." Here's what Biggus and his friends did.

Through an inside contact, Biggus and friends located the unclaimed corpse of a hooker who had died of a heart attack—yeah, for real. She was flashy, about forty, and built about 43-30-37. She was also quite dead.

Biggus says, "We had Rev. Jerkwad doing the service in his own church—what a con. It was closed coffin, and I was in my suit and crying. Then, in the middle of the eulogy, two mourners stood up and began to argue about which one she loved best.

"They took off their jackets, as if to fight, and by golly, they were not wearing shirts, just tattoos, muscles, and dog collars. They were using loud, gross language to describe the sexual stuff each did with the deceased."

At this point, as Rev. Jerkwad sputtered to silence and the crowd was oohing and ahhing, Biggus stood up and said, "Let's see what she thinks."

He opened the coffin to display the corpse dressed in skimpy leather and other very kinky apparel that displayed her hefty bosoms and prominent genitalia. Biggus also pointed out to the crowd how her pubic hair was shaved in a heart shape.

"I shouted to the crowd, 'Anyone have a camera? Let's get some good fun pictures . . . kind of a last porno thing for old-time's sake for my dear auntie here!' People began to leave Jerkwad's church."

OK, OK, if that's too strong for you, consider that you could also have some fun with your least favorite mark/preacher at a funeral by putting an inappropriate T-shirt on the deceased or a bumper sticker on the casket.

GIFTS

My old comrade Commodore Simon Tuggmutton described a wedding as a ceremony not so well disguised that you cannot smell your own funeral flowers. Yet, as Johnny Yount once pointed out, you can have a lot of fun with the invitations to such an event.

As all of us who've attended weddings know, it takes a long, long time for thank-you notes to arrive. Indeed, I am still waiting for such notes about my gifts at the last wedding of the late Alice Roosevelt Longworth, which I attended.

Brother Yount has a grand solution. He knew a friend who tired of waiting for the expected "thank-you" note and decided to help the newlyweds by writing notes in their behalf. That is a fine Christian attitude. Here is a sample card:

Thank you so much for your satisfactory gift. Biffy and I will appreciate it forever and think of you often. However, someone of your financial means and supposed good taste should have chosen a whole lot better and perhaps even spent a few more dollars to assure quality. But, we do appreciate your gesture anyway.

Naturally, this note is written to match the bride's handwriting as closely as possible.

Thinking ahead, Johnny thought of sending premature wedding invitations, too, with incorrect dates, times, locations, perhaps even incorrect people. He suggests you could also mention a mandatory minimum price for a gift.

GRAFFITI

In The Magic Z's neighborhood, a teenage punk penis-head turned graffiti into the squall of the wild. Z says this punk kid was always defacing the property of others with spray paint. This created a hardship for a lot of older folks on fixed pensions who lived in the neighborhood. Z and two friends decided to help this jerk clean up his act.

As it was near to Halloween time, the avengers decided to soap the bad kid's car windows. But, then, they thought, why stop there? Let's really clean things up for this defacer of others' property.

Z reports, "We didn't just use regular hand soap, either. We created a mixture of Borax, Spic & Span, Ajax, and a couple of industrial-strength cleaners heavy on bleach. We added just enough water to make a rough, coarse paste.

"Our next step was to get his car, the only possession of which he could be proud, and proceeded to 'soap' it thoroughly. And, I do mean we were thorough. We 'soaped' it all over, every surface, inside and out."

Considering that Z lives in a pretty dry climate, this paste created some real problems for the pricky punk's car. Z says he understands that this mixture was so strong that it actually restored the vehicle's finish to its original pre-painted format in many spots. I suspect that this sort of cleansing would do wonders for the interior, too, possibly cleaning the leather right off the seats.

But the main result is that the kid has been so busy with his own problems that he and his spray paint haven't hassled any of the other folks in the neighborhood.

◆

Obviously, that was not your typical George Hayduke graffiti story. It was more of a counter-graffiti story. For traditionalists, here is something more familiar, examples of new graffiti I have seen across this and other countries recently. As always, you're welcome to share your graffiti with me (see The Last Word for details).
- SHIT HAPPENS . . . EXXON'S LIFE STORY
- WILL THE LAST AMERICAN TO LEAVE (name the city of your choice) PLEASE BRING OUR FLAG OUT, TOO?
- THE (fill in the person or group of your choice) IS LIKE A SORE DICK, NOT WORTH SHIT AND YOU CAN'T BEAT IT.
- VULGARITY IS THE GARLIC IN THE SALAD OF TASTE.
- IS THERE LIFE BEFORE DEATH?

- THE GREAT SEEM GREAT ONLY BECAUSE WE ARE ON OUR KNEES.
- CANCER CURES SMOKING.
- A WOMAN NEEDS A MAN (or vice versa) LIKE A FISH NEEDS A BICYCLE.

GUN GRABBERS

Many folks who support the stupidity of restrictive gun laws in the false hope that this will decrease crime, violence, and death are misguided idealists, intellectual lotus eaters who don't understand the truly shitty nature of our politicians and bureaucrats. Others in the gun-banning business are police state dictators, fascist-minded megacop personalities with political ambition, or professional fund-raisers and con artists who leech money from these media-attractive groups.

Reading their literature and seeing their leaders on television, their misinformed lies pass through my mind quickly, like undigested corn being shit out of a horse. In addition to the high fecal factor of their rhetoric, they are useful marks for a lot of easy fun. So are their media cronies, most of whom fear firearms and therefore are against them.

The Rogue suggests that pro-gun stickers would go well on the bumper or the rear deck of a notorious antigunner's vehicle. Another of our folks, Princess Charlene, attended a few of the antigun gatherings in her area and placed stickers reading SUPPORT THE NRA, THIS CAR PROTECTED BY SMITH & WESSON, and I SUCK GUN BARRELS on the vehicles of the antigun gurus in charge of the meetings.

Another of Princess Charlene's helpful hints involves birthdays. This bright, active lady pays attention to the birthdays of antigun folks and their kids and always sends gift-wrapped shirts to them from the various national progun groups.

"My kicker is that I send T-shirts with a picture of a sniper rifle that say things like REACH OUT AND TOUCH SOMEONE, or I enclose a shirt with the logo of a firearms manufacturer," she adds.

"The best part, so I hear from my spies, is that the kids really like the shirts and wear them or raise hell if their folks say no."

The Rogue likes to leave war toys and toy guns around the yard of an antigunner with little kids. He says that the kids will find the toys and play with them. They will resent the parents who get furious and take them away. Ahhh, the pied pistolero and pistolera live!

HALLOWEEN

Halloween used to be a fun time for kids. I suppose it still is, but I think the adults who sell and rent expensive costumes to parents probably achieve the most profitable pleasure. When my peers were kids a big part of the season was carving a jack-o'-lantern from a big, ripe pumpkin... part of lost folklore, I guess.

Also part of that childhood folklore are the ubiquitous neighborhood bullies who came around after you were in bed and smashed your jack-o'-lantern to smithereens. In a few earlier books, I presented ways in which various folks have made this prank painful for bullies.

To date, though, Ryan has the best plan I've heard. Here's how he gets instant payback on the pumpkin killers.

"My first stop is the hobby shop to buy a package of electric matches, those little devices used to safely ignite model rocket engines," Ryan explains, adding, "they produce an explosive flame when exposed to electric current."

At another shop, Ryan purchased a package of

thick green fuze of the type used with fireworks. Using a standard nine-volt battery and some thin wire, he hooked the various components together to a firecracker.

"Fireworks are illegal, so if you don't have them or can't make them, use an emergency road flare. The idea is to hook it up so that when a switch is thrown, the electric match ignites the fuze, which ignites the exploding device. You can attach the thin speaker wire to your switch if you like."

His next step was to place the entire assembly inside a large, hollowed-out pumpkin that had been rigged with a pressure switch so that when the pumpkin was picked up, the switch tripped, igniting the electric match and so forth.

Ryan adds, "I first did this a few years ago and sure enough, some redneck peckerhead comes goofing along and picks up my pumpkin, carries it out from my porch toward the street, ready to hoist it over his head to smash on the sidewalk when the big baby exploded, showering pumpkin mess all over him."

Ryan says that the kid wasn't burned or hurt, just scared shitless, perhaps literally, plus he was covered with pumpkin goo. Naturally, neighbors all came running to see what had happened.

"It was very rewarding to see this big pumpkin-bashing bully sitting there on the street all goo'd and shitted up, crying like a baby 'cause he was so scared. Later, I heard that he had, indeed, shit his pants, plus his parents grounded him big-time because of all the embarrassment he'd caused."

Happy Halloween, kiddies.

◆

Meanwhile, the erstwhile Virginia Aldertree reported that some trick or treaters from her neighborhood came home from a mall-planned Halloween promotion with tiny, sample-sized packs of flavored sex lubricants in with their candy and other treats.

"It seems someone had a grudge against the mall and had brought in a carton of the samples, professionally imprinted on one side with the mall logo, and had a clown-dressed person handing them out in the mall for about fifteen minutes, moving all the time," Ginny told me.

Happy Halloween, everyone.

HIJACKING

A criminal is usually someone with all the aggressive instincts of greed, dishonesty, and a predatory nature, yet who lacks the funding to run for office or form a corporation. Sometimes the smarter folks also realize that the tradecraft of the criminal is also useful to the vengeful soul. It's the same situation whereby one person's freedom fighter is another's terrorist, i.e., the actors and motives may differ, but the tactics and results are the same.

That sermonette introduces you to the charming Kieu Mayate, a young lady I met outside the United States, who told me a sad story of her brief life in North America. She had been married to a truck driver who abused her before leaving her for many other women, finally settling on one. I was astonished when I saw a photo of the other woman sitting in a bar with Kieu's ex. In contrast to the gorgeous, sweet Kieu, this other woman looked like a toilet plunger sitting on a barstool. My astonishment showed.

"Drugs," was Kieu's simple answer.

It seems this woman's brother was a major middleman who was looking for wheeled transport for his product. Hence, Kieu's ex-sweetie saw far more vision of a pot of gold than another honeypot, albeit a repulsive one.

Kieu's family came to the States and then into Mexico to help. Basically, what they did was move their truck ahead of the mark, Kieu's ex, identified themselves as being the ex, and spirited the load away.

Guess who was in a whole shitpot full of hurt? Obviously, this little object lesson from Kieu is worthy of your perusal. The same scam can be used for any means of transport or product. Or you can run a reverse hijack and blame it on the mark as well. As noted before, the machinations and modifications of this scam are limited only by your imagination and assertiveness.

HOME

My good friend Enoch Pruid used to live with a certain Ms. Ferkel until he caught her once too often making their apartment into her sexual convenience store for the neighborhood. You guessed it, Ferkel was not real serious about relationships, and Enoch didn't like sleeping on other guys' wet spots.

They had a major falling out, and she ordered him out of their place. As her new steady was a cop, she told Enoch if he tried to take anything like "their" tapes or other joint property, she'd have his ass tossed in the slammer for molesting her and all the nuns in the city—stuff like that.

Enoch took just his basics and left. But, he also did something else—some final home maintenance that you might find amusing or even useful.

"I made a pasty mixture of table salt and water, undid the cover plates on all of the electrical connections, and coated them. I knew I'd be long gone and forgotten when the corrosion finally hit," Enoch explained.

Better yet, he told me later, it seems that just before the corrosion bomb he left had exploded, Enoch learned that Ms. Ferkel had a falling out with her cop friend and ordered him out of their apartment. The cop took the heat for the electric hassles.

One guesses that the spark has gone out of that romance.

◆

The Magic Z has a fine stunt for your mark's chimney. Buy or make a twenty-foot strand of firecrackers. Get on the mark's roof and carefully lower the strand down the chimney . . . preferably when there is not a fire in the fireplace. Tie the other end to the chimney top.

When the mark lights his fire and it starts to roar, it will ignite the string of firecrackers. Mr. Magic's after-action report from his test case said, "It made the entire side of the house shake, blew sparks all over, and made the family evacuate and call the fire department. And, we used tiny little crackers."

◆

From blow to grow, it seems that many modern marks are using nature to decorate with now, which makes our work a lot easier. Dastardly Dan apparently agreed because he suggested that you help your mark decorate his home by including a living anthill in an artistically rewarding location.

"I think the middle of the living room would be fine, or in a bedroom, perhaps in the bed itself," Dan suggests.

As an added-value idea, why not semihide the surprise gift until its inhabitants have had a chance to not only explore but to multiply and occupy, e.g., put the anthill in a storage area, the attic, or a loft . . . somewhere it won't be noticed for a few days or so.

HOOKERS

A friend of mine in the publishing business once told me that hiring a prostitute was like having a mistress on a piecework basis. However, while it's a hooker's job to get screwed, it's also possible to have a helpful hooker help you to screw your mark. Mike R. from L.A. did just that.

Mike says, "This guy was a real dirtbag, a nasty, mean bastard whose bragging mouth ruined the reputation of several young ladies about whose sexual appetite for him he had lied. Following your method of the punishment fitting the crime, George, we used sex to pay him back."

Mike obtained the services of a friendly prostitute with a sense of humor and justice who worked in a not-so-nearby city. She called the mark's parents to complain about their son's sexual abuse and to inform them that she was filing a paternity suit against him. She claimed she was pregnant by him and would prove it in court.

"The best part is that the smartass had never even met this lady. He had no idea what was going on," Mike said with a grin. "He was really glazed after his parents lit into him. But we weren't done. Using a legal-form guidebook, we drew up a reasonable facsimile of the suit papers, made fake notary seals on them, and mailed them to the guy's parents."

For their finale, Mike and friends borrowed a copy of the guy's high-school yearbook portrait and a nice picture of the hooker, wrote a brief, realistic-sounding engagement announcement, and then paid thirty dollars to have it inserted in their local newspaper. Incredibly, the newspaper never verified any of this information. It ran the engagement notice with both photos.

According to Mike, rumor, humor, and a whole lot of nasty confusion and anger were swapped around the community for months afterward.

◆

Tommie Titmouse suggests a more passive way to use prostitution to have fun with a mark. Tommie says this one works best for a female mark, but I can also see a lot of humor here if your mark is male.

Prostitution is legal in Nevada. There are several directories published commercially that list these legal poof houses, sort of like a diner's guide, you might say. Tommie's idea is to have your mark apply for employment. Naturally, you will need to create a catchy résumé, a come-on cover letter, and a *wow* photo. You're clever, you figure that one out.

My twist to this would be to apply for your male mark. Only his letter should emphasize that the owners would make more money if they were a full-service house. Have the mark inform them that he is a switch-hitter.

Some interesting correspondence could come from this neon-starred profusion of syphilitic delights.

ID CARDS

My friendly Texas pal, Joan, used to date a nasty cabby whose constants included lying, cheating, and stealing. Often she was the victim. But, she says that payback, far from being a bitch, was real fun for her. Here's her story.

"One of my fun stunts was to make up new ID cards for him—you know, those official ID cards with photo, description, and all, that are put up facing the backseat."

Joan "borrowed" an original card blank from the issuing authority and with her art, computer, and creative talents, designed a whole series of new cards for her least favorite cabby. She would sometimes substitute a picture of a different race or gender person for his photo. Or, she might put in some unlikely name, such as Richard Nixon, Al Capone, Ho Chi Minh, or the like.

"Sometimes I would use his real picture and name, then in the description lines write messages like 'I eat pussy,' or 'I kiss little boys,' or, 'I can see your snatch,' or, 'I just ate a booger sandwich,' stuff like that."

Joan says she switched cards nightly for three weeks before he caught on. She says he used to wonder why so many of his passengers either seemed to be highly insulted or highly amused all of the time, as well as why his tips were down. Joan says she was always highly amused by all of this, and, being the caring lady that she is, she decided to share the humor with you.

IN PRIVITY

As Mahng Tia says, "Give me thirty seconds with your car and not only will I learn your life, I can ruin it." What we're getting at here is a legal term known as "in privity," which, for our purposes here, means learning all you can about a mark from a vehicle identification number (VIN). The VIN for each vehicle is usually on the driver's-side dash, always visible from the outside.

Mahng Tia says, "You simply call the state Department of Motor Vehicles, tell the clerk you are John from John's Towing in (name some town), and that the owner of this car (give mark's VIN) owes you storage fees and may have used phony ID, and that you need to file a lien. You need the owner's name, address, and other registration information."

In all fifty states that sort of information is public, but most clerks and cops are too lazy to look it up for an ordinary citizen. Thus, you put yourself inside the law-enforcement loop, e.g., John's Towing. You also need to know the names of other lienholders, which is likely on new cars (banks or loan companies, for example), plus the operator's license number and date of birth. Tell the clerk that you (John's Towing) got a bad check that doesn't match the mark's ID. Since you're in the loop, the clerk will give you these data.

Now that you have a driver's license number, name, and date of birth, you call the state driver's license bureau, and this time you are (choose a fun name) from the Roxie School of Charm. You then tell the clerk that the mark (use Mark's name) has applied to you for a job, and you're checking legal liability information. You give the clerk the mark's name, date of birth, license number, and all of that good data you got from your last call. You tell the clerk you want to know if Mark is legally employable—does s/he have a Social Security number? Tell the clerk that Mark left that information off the employment form. The clerk will read the mark's Social Security number to you.

Congratulations, you are now "in privity," as those in the criminal injustice system would say. Depending upon how each state system works, you now have a tremendous range of personal data on your mark. The uses for this information are limited only by your lack of imagination and determination. Indeed, in some of the other sections of this book, I will touch on some of the specific uses that Mahng Tia has mentioned from time to time, such as credit.

IRS

Joker once had a real love, a woman he thought he could live with for life. Turned out she was megaslut, an entire tourist attraction in herself. She was the type who'd honk the holy man's Johnson and wink while communion was being served. When Joker learned of her carnal misdeeds, he found out that she was fornicating her employer's business expenses as well.

Being a good citizen, Joker says he contacted the Internal Revenue Service (IRS) to report that his ex-sweetie was not only a tax cheat, but a crook as well. He says, "I did this through two good and proper citizens, although they didn't know it at the time. Both were married businessmen with whom my lady had partied."

Did I neglect to inform you that Joker is a highly skilled forger? Sorry. He also wasn't done with this superwhore whose honesty, ethics, and morals were lower than Nixon's soul.

"My next stunt was to publish a little booklet titled 'Kick the IRS in the Balls.' It was full of truly radical advice on how to screw the IRS out of tax money. I got some of the ideas from your books, George, and the rest was really rotten stuff I got from a retired IRS employee who's a good friend."

His booklet included instructions on diverting IRS mail, sabotaging IRS offices, using the mail to harass IRS employees, plus hinting at kidnapping, forgery, and other illegal deeds. The booklet concluded with a militant invitation to join this radical No More Taxes League. Joker used his ex-lover's name, address, and telephone number at the end of the message as headquarters for the league.

"I put copies on the windshield of every car in the two malls in my city area, in supermarkets, at the local minor-league ball park, and in apartment complex mailboxes," Joker related.

Oh, before I forget, Joker wants me to reassure you that all of the above is complete fiction, total imagination, and all in good, spirited humor. He really didn't actually do any of that stuff, he was just goofing on us all.

JAIL

Forget government and the clergy, the best place to find people with true convictions is in jail. Our Texas fixer, Biggus Piraphicus, cheered as his town's official bully was finally locked up after getting nailed for one of his dozens of crimes against civilized people. Of course, there are some civilized folks in Texas, so stop snickering.

Old Biggus thought he might add some spice to this stew of incarceration in which his nemesis found himself. Biggus bought a real cheap used gun and a box of shells at a flea market. He disassembled the weapon and wrapped it and the ammo carefully. He then mailed it to the bully in jail, with the bully's kid brother's return address.

If you don't like guns, then you can mail a knife, hatchet, machete, drugs, or any legal no no. At last word, Biggus, who went to school with the local police chief's daughter, thought he might create some porno picture composites from old school photos and mail them to the chief—"from" bully boy.

As any con knows, if you have money or

trade goods you can get anything in jail or prison, from dope to weapons to a VCR to the USS *Iowa*. I'm not sure about that last one. I'll have to ask my good buddy and co-conspirator Admiral Dick Milligan. But, you get my point.

◆

  Merwyn E. Bogue tells me of a payback involving a young prisoner who had been framed for an inside theft by an older, more experienced con. It added six months to the kid's already stupid ten-month sentence for smoking a joint.
  After his release, the kid bided his time. He told Merwyn, "This guy was a slug and a physical coward. Ugly, too, his momma probably used tongs to carry him around for the first few years. What I did was to write a real mash note to the jail-house stud, a big surly sumbitch who could carry a full-grown bull under each arm. He was filthy, too. You could have raised mushrooms in the decay on his front teeth alone. His breath would have clogged the sinuses of a giraffe . . . you getting the picture?" The note was "from" the swine who'd framed the kid. The kid paid to have it smuggled into the slammer and delivered to the animal as if it had come from the framer.
  I'll leave the details, as Merwyn explained them to me, of what happened next to your imagination. If you remember the film *Deliverance,* you have a clue, and if you have an X-rated imagination for violent, deviant sexual action, well—as the Koran points out—one sword is worth ten thousand words.

JOCKS

Ahh, this is a field I know well, having been one of this species before I became the sensitive, caring human being that I am today. Mike R. from L.A. helped deal a double whammy a few years back, sacking both an obnoxious, small-town TV sportscaster and an obnoxious, small-other-town high school jock/jerk. I suspect the word obnoxious in the last sentence is redundant in both instances.

Mike said the kid was from a nearby town and deserved payback for his bullying ways. This jock had been suspended from the basketball team for three games for beating up a real student. Meanwhile, the small-town TV station a few dozen miles away was too cheap to hire stringers and relied on free student help: "Be a junior jock sniffer" kind of thing whereby a student manager or other dweeb called in the score for his school.

Mike reports, "We had a sexy babe, one of my buddy's cousins from another school, waylay this basketball student manager on this way to phone in the score of the game. While she flirted with him, one of our guys called in our version of the story.

"We had the locals beating the shit out of their bigtime rival—which wasn't even the team they played—even though the locals had lost to another team. We had the suspended player scoring a league-high fifty-seven points and even conned the jerk sportscaster into doing a phone interview with one of our guys who claimed to be this jock.

"Meantime, we made sure that the dweebie manager couldn't get back in time to phone in the real story by planning a car breakdown for him. Everything worked for us, so all of the wrong information got on the eleven o'clock news that night."

Mike says the phony story kicked up a whole shitstorm of complaints. He adds that he and his friends called the station and the school to complain. As one neat sidebar to all of this, the parents of the banned jock "star" of the game threatened to sue the sportscaster, the station, and the school for mental distress. Mike said he and some of his pals wrote letters to the local paper urging support for this action.

Mike reports that one of the true benefits of this stunt—after all of the confusion, bullshit, and rancor had been sorted and sifted—was that his school took a new, more realistic attitude toward athletics.

JUNQUE MAIL

Airwolf has been having some true mail mental pause problems, as in junque mail and poor service with his real mail. Ever the cheerful sort, he offers a couple of solutions for your consideration. For instance, to counter chain letters, he includes custom-copied composite porno pictures, rewrites the letter, then sends along the revised edition, using the address of a deserving mark for the "last name" return.

He also discovered the postal bar code at the bottom of many junque mail letters and how it is used. Airwolf suggests that you use a Magic Marker or a similar device to alter the bars. Like everything else connected with our postal service, this bar-code editing is highly illegal.

◆

Airwolf is not alone, though, in his mail altercation/alteration. A very good friend, The Mountain Homesteader, gets really upset with pressure groups using junque mail to pester him for money, especially when he gets requests from groups representing views he can't stand.

"For example, like you, George, I'm a very strong believer in the right to freely own and use firearms," Homesteader says. "When I get mail from these antigun liars, I get nasty."

He really does. I know this man. He is a bright, gentle, quiet pacifist, but when he gets angry, well . . .

"I took the return envelope from one of those idiot gun-grabber groups and had a printer make several hundred copies. I gave them to friends and suggested that each friend mail a box of rocks, sand, gravel, or anything heavy to these bozos. That way they get to pay the postage," my friend said.

It's a perfect ploy for any pressure group. Mr. Homesteader does offer a caution, though. He says not to send dirty diapers, body parts, or animal/human waste. That would violate health laws. Also, never send anything that the police could possibly construe as threatening. That is a major-league felony. For example, do not send simulated bombs, alarm clocks, ammunition, junked gun parts, or other such devices.

Remember, the idea here is to make your mark pay out his or her money needlessly. Your goal is *not* to threaten anyone. Specifics? At today's postal rates, a two-pound box will cost the mark about three dollars, while ten pounds of contribution will cost between eight and thirteen dollars.

◆

The Magic Z knew a jerk who polluted our world by carelessly tossing beer and soda cans all over the streets. To help this jerk see his errors, Magic Z collected the mark's junque mail for two months until he had a bag full of it. "Next, I dumped all of the mail into a city sewer, making sure it was a dry week with no rain. Next, from a pay phone, I made a 'concerned-citizen' call to the city street department and reported that I'd seen someone dump a whole bag of litter down a storm sewer," Magic Z explained.

In an hour, city workers had found the dumped junque mail. Guess whose name and address were on everything? Soon, the police were visiting the mark's house.

So, you see, junque mail can be useful. It just depends upon what it contains and where it is deposited.

KIDDIES

When asked how he liked children, W.C. Fields replied, "Parboiled." Actually, like a good utility cut of meat, children are far more versatile than that and may be served accordingly. For example, my Texas pal Biggus Piraphicus suggests that you can get to your mark through his or her marklings. I'm not talking nasty stuff like death squads do; I'm talking Hayduke fun here.

Consider that you could get your mark's kids a loud musical instrument, such as drums or an electric guitar. Or, you may wish to send the little ones explicit porno in the name of some secondary mark, family or otherwise. Biggus also suggests that you see that they get supplies of placebos that look like illegal drugs. Did you note Biggus' use of passive voice in that last sentence? I did.

Some years ago, I gave the child of a favored mark an unusual pet on several special occasions, including a large goose for her birthday, a porcupine for Easter, a skunk for Mother's Day, and a family of huge Belgian rabbits for Christmas. I am certain the symbolism of these gifts is not lost on quicker readers. No matter the symbolism, the mark was stuck with more than that.

◆

Speaking of children, I just now remembered Fishface Haller, an acquaintance from high school, and how he and Izzy Ferkel used to locate medium-sized, relatively fresh roadkill and stuff them into the musical instruments of their marks—sneaky little snitches who always toadied up to teachers by squealing on the class clowns. Ahhh, the glorious days of high school.

◆

While experimenting with various products, including red pepper and other delightful spices, Mello Smello learned that not only will it keep obnoxious relatives' or friends' obnoxious pets unhappy with your digs, little kiddies also have negative memories of your pepper house from hell.

Mr. Smello explains, "I was running some reaction experiments with red pepper in an attempt to keep the gawdamn cats off my back fence, when the muse struck me about trying red pepper on my carpets when an unruly dog is visiting. It worked."

As a side benefit, he also found that unruly rugrats became very vocal in their attempts to quit the premises. He added that the pepper is easily swept up after the animals leave.

"I found these obnoxious visitors had a long memory regarding my place and didn't come back. For that, I bless you, red pepper," says Mello Smello.

LANDLORDS

Even though he felt like he was living in the unproverbial straw shithouse, Mike R. from L.A. stayed in his same place because it was close to work. But, his one-room apartment was dirty, old, and smelled like a used rendering plant. His landlord refused to do any maintenance or pay for any cleanup or repair. He told Mike, "If you want it, you do it. If you don't like it, move."

The straw that broke the brick came when the landlord let his two cousins live in the apartment while Mike was in Europe for several weeks. It didn't seem possible, but these two slobs added the meaning of pigsty and town dump to the earlier description Mike gave to the place.

"To top it off, the landlord told me he was holding me responsible for any damages when I left," Mike said. "My security deposit was only fifty dollars, so I figured I'd get some help from two pals and here's what we did just before I left the place.

"One of the guys got 2,800 discarded bricks free from a building demolition site. After I'd packed everything of mine and moved, all without notifying the landlord, my buddies and I spent part of a day and all night redecorating the entire apartment."

What Mike and his friends did was brick the entire interior of the dingy apartment. They did it to "cover up the mess and stench and to make a home improvement," he said. They used mortar to brick every surface, floor to ceiling, wall to wall, then the floor itself.

They kept the door shut and the blinds down, so nobody knew what was going on. They also pulled their caper when the neighbors from the nearby two apartments were away for the weekend. Mike told me he figures the gross weight of the brickwork was about 9,300 pounds.

"The story I got months later from a friend was that Mr. Landlord had to spend a couple of grand and a lot of time, including some guys with jackhammers, to break up the mess. The other neighbors were far more pissed at him than at me. And, I was long, long gone to nobody knew where, except my pals, and Mr. Landlord didn't know them," Mike added.

Mike said he was glad the apartment was on the ground floor because the weight of the bricks might have collapsed the floor and hurt people below. And he added that carrying all of those bricks upstairs would have been tiring and created unwanted attention.

◆

Just as Mike had a scumlord, there is also the other side, the decent landlord who has derelicts as renters. Rick from Tampa told me about just such a case. The renters were dishonest, stupid, low-life scum who were always in trouble and unable to hold jobs, but, unfortunately, able to breed: they had passed along their defective genes to four kids. We'll call these slimes the Arschlochs. They were six months behind in their rent and had caused more than eight times their security deposit in damages in only a year's time.

Rick says that when they left town for a three-week visit with her family, the landlord, Mr. Niceguy, was thrilled to get into his furnished house, which they were ruining. He called the Salvation Army in the next city and had them come to the home and strip everything out of it.

Next, he had the entire house professionally cleaned, painted, and papered. He put in new shrubbery and trees. And, as a final touch, with only five days to spare, he rented it to a real nice young family, the Happyfaces.

When the Arschlochs returned, they were totally bewildered but too stupid to completely understand what had happened. Both Mr. Niceguy and Mr. Happyface insisted that they had never seen the Arsloch family before. In Mr. Happyface's case, it was totally true. In Mr. Niceguy's case, it was delightful revenge.

"Mr. Niceguy told the Arschlochs that he had no idea who they were and that they'd never lived there. He also told them he would call the police if they persisted in bothering him or the Happyfaces," Rick said.

LAUNDRY

The sad truth is that we can't often pick our workplace associates. Thus, the gods of fate often amuse themselves by sodomizing us with less than desirable on-the-job associates. When Robin was working in the rather closed environment of the military, he was forced to share laundry facilities with a jerk who hogged the machines.

Everyone hated the guy, Robin relates, because when they tried to reason with him about sharing, human relations, and all of that, he remained a selfish, arrogant bully who thought only of himself.

"I thought he was a firebomb of rage and needed to be hosed down," Robin remembers. "So, I decided to help him with his laundry. I added a quart of liquid bleach and a quart of AFFF foam concentrate to his laundry detergent."

In the interest of the serious-minded scholars among you, a thimbleful of AFFF concentrate will fill a sink with this fire-retarding foam.

I leave the result of Robin's wash-day assistance to your imagination, although he did report that the laundry facility was neck deep in foam and that the washer-hog was held responsible for the damages.

    Good hosing, Robin. I trust you also stood by to piss on him.

MAIL

The U.S. Post Office and its product, mail, are a big part of the creative Hayduker's stamping grounds. Many of my past books have featured numerous ways you can use and abuse the U.S. mail. However, care must be taken because, as I've stated in the past, the postal cops play rough and dirty.

The wonderful New Age Lady offers some excellent advice when doing Haydukery postal things on behalf of your marks.

- Use generic stamps or prestamped envelopes bought from the USPS in another city.
- Use someone else's typewriter and/or word processor.
- Buy separate supplies for your actions, such as paper, envelopes, and pens. Don't use the same supplies that you use for your mail.
- Don't work out of your home or office. Use someone else's or a neutral location (try the library) so nothing can be traced back to you.
- Wear gloves.

If you're considering a mail-forwarding service, New Age Lady recommends selecting one from a supermarket tabloid. These companies don't ask questions; they just want your money and will remail for you. If you select a fancy one that advertises in the yellow pages, be advised that they require USPS forms to be completed and will probably not keep your identity a secret from postal inspectors. Other sources for a useful remailing service can be found in alternative magazines and newspapers.

I'd add here that you need to be careful, as The Just Us Department Gestapo and the postal police run stings to entrap folks like you all the time. Why you? First, you're reading this book. Second, you're not rich and don't have an expensive lawyer who's in the old-boy loop. Third, it doesn't matter if you *voted* for Reagan or Bush. How much money did you give them?

Be warned: rather than getting big government off our backs as promised, Ron and George have them walking all over our personal rights, lives, and property. That's something I'd like to stamp out and cancel.

MARK

As in my other books, I use the word *mark* to refer to the object of your revenge. A mark can be a person, institution, company, animal, object—just about anything that has hurt you in any manner or continues to do so. Usually, you've tried all of the ethical, legal, moral, and Golden Rule things to make everyone happy. You're a paragon of patience, a vigor of virtue. But your mark is a true anus stain and won't stop bullying, annoying, or bothering you.

This is when you begin to get angry. You're getting so frustrated and angry that you want to watch a rabid moray eel eat the mark's eyeballs—while the mark is still alive. Or you feel as if your mark needs to be in the nearest intensive-care unit.

Hold those thoughts, because that's when it's time to call on George Hayduke, bullybuster. Within the pages of this book, you'll discover all sorts of bullybusting ideas, ranging from the mildly sardonic to the bombastically devastating.

But, as a matter of early warning intelligence,

how can you spot a potential mark? Thanks to some exhaustive research at the Hayduke Institute of Semiological Research, Dr. Bruno McManmon, project director, has come up with some characteristics that fit a computer-generated model to profile myriad marks. This profile indicates that a potential mark:

• thinks that when she/he defecates, the odor of lilacs fills the stalls;
• is the sort of person for whom it would be redundant to claim ignorance;
• often carries that rotten-guilty look, like a nasty little boy who's peed his pants;
• has all of the sexual appeal of rancid lard;
• has a foul personality that stands out like a neon cockroach in a bowl of grits;
• blows dead bears for a quarter and gives change;
• would sell his/her grandmother to a Nigerian brothel if the price were right;
• has the personality of week-old sinus drainage;
• has the ethical standards of a Bolivian drug dealer selling poisoned heroin to kids in your neighborhood.

I could go on, but I suspect you get the drift. A mark is someone you want to come down on to make your neighborhood a nicer place to live. Nothing wrong with that.

Remember, for your mark, your revenge has to be his or her season in hell. Consider *Hamlet*, Act II, Scene 2, "O God, I could be bounded in a nutshell and count myself a king of infinite space, were it not that I have bad dreams." You want your mark to have bad dreams, especially those dreams that end with: *it could happen again, asshole!*

Marks are all around us, although there are statistically few of them when compared to the nice folk. It's your choice whether to respond to or ignore your mark. As the offended, you must choose who to fricassee on the hot coals of their ill-chosen act or words. So, to all of the marks in your life, I offer a curse from an old shaman I knew in another life in a dark, evil section of a small island south of the United States:

"The death fart from a terrified adult is a thousand times worse than anything a live body can emit. May such a death fart multiply a thousand times in the nostrils of your enemy."

—Moloch Beelzebub
Hinchazon Cay, 1980

MILITARY

One of the finer things about our military system is its consistency over the past umpteen generations. Whatever the cause, just or otherwise, the major conclusion will be the same: either massive physical destruction or the creation of locally franchised bars and brothels. This, in turn, encourages the spread of corruption, disease, greed, and other bad shit.

Allen, who was in the military when he wrote, suggested a couple of fun items to play games with your fellow service personnel. One is to learn to forge signatures, then to file a DA Form 4187, which is a request for Personnel Action.

You request a transfer for your mark to some awful duty station. Of course, it won't go through. That's not the point. The point is that 1) an investigation will occur, and 2) your mark will be a major part of it. The military works that way. Even if innocent, your mark will carry the stigma on his record, not to mention the gossip trail among the regulars.

As Allen notes, if you do this right, you will

never be involved. But, your mark's name is now "known" in connection with a problem. In the military, that is not a good situation.

Another of Allen's ideas is to fake a duty roster. This will cause all sorts of delays, problems, irritations, complaints, investigations, and suspicions. Depending upon your mark, you can get lots of people into hassles with this one.

◆

As a generic stunt, I recall an old pal who'd been in Special Forces for most of his tours telling gleeful tales about how they doctored medical supplies with various viruses and germs, then allowed them to fall into the hands of the Viet Cong. That's medicine for an old sick soul, eh?

◆

Former Sgt. Elmo Pcod took a lot of personal crap from his boss, a turd lifer named MSgt. Remf. Remf used "the book" to make Pcod's assignment miserable. Pcod requested and received a transfer to a new unit.

Before this happened, Pcod discovered something useful. It seems that Remf was a fitness nut and sometimes sought a secluded area off post to work out, sometimes bringing along some bimbette or trainee bimbo.

"Having photographic equipment, talent, and imagination, I shot some telephoto pictures of that asshole Remf and one of his cuties, both in the buff, posing all over each other," Pcod said.

Ever the prudent man, Pcod saved these photos for nearly a year. Then, he had a nonmilitary friend write some very hot 'n' horny lust letters to the seventeen-year-old daughter of the base commanding general, asking her to join his friend and him for a three-way physical workout. The letter was signed with a fair approximation of MSgt. Remf's handwriting. Two pictures accompanied the letter.

Pcod made no inquiry, but heard through the NCO-vine that big rumbles came down on unfortunate MSgt. Remf.

MY SLOGAN

Many friends ask me what the Latin slogan at the bottom of my letterhead means. That slogan, *oderint dum metuant*, means, "Let them hate, provided they fear." One of my technical research friends, Bob Burnham, tells me that this motto was originally attributed to Tiberius, Roman emperor from 14-37 A.D. Interestingly, the same basic slogan in German was used by Heinrich Himmler for Nazi political propaganda purposes.

As a multilingual scholar, Bob notes, "I don't remember the German wording precisely, but it struck me as more impressive than the Latin. But, Hitler was more impressive than Tiberius, too."

Thanks, too, to Latin research expert Eugene Ehrlich and Germanic scholar LTC Martin N. McGeary, Jr., USA, Retd.

NEIGHBORS

Ever live next to uncaring neighbors who like to ram-start, then loudly *revvv* their cars' engines while you're trying to sleep, no matter what the clock or calendar says? You might enjoy The Professor's thoughts on that.

"I worked late with night classes and reading papers, then had to get to school at seven the next morning. Yet, these next-door camheads raced their cars at three or four in the morning, whenever they felt like it. I asked them nicely to stop, explaining why. They just laughed."

The Professor waited until a good Ohio winter to get back at the Bozo Brothers and their loud car. He fought their fiery noise with icy calm.

"When they finally would go to bed, I'd turn on a garden hose, theirs, by the way, and spray water on their driveway and all over their car. Naturally, I did this only on nights it snowed, sleeted, and was very awful out there."

As he lived in Snowbelt, Ohio, that was often.

When the Bozo Brothers would try to get into their ice-locked car to start it, all sorts of fun took place, not to mention much taking of the Lord's name in vain. If they did manage to get into the vehicle, get it started, then try to roar out of the driveway, they would discover the inch of solid ice under the fresh snowfall.

The Professor said that one fine morning he enjoyed watching his gnarly neighbors slam their car into a tree, careen off that, and into their other car, which was up on blocks. On another occasion, they slid the icemobile down a short grade and into a field where it sat for three days until they could get it towed out. "They didn't figure what was wrong for the longest time, just kept gunning and slip-sliding away. It was a fun, fun winter for me."

He adds that when the light of reason did go on in the dimbulbs' brains, their vehicular activities became more civil.

NUCLEAR

Whoever says that politics is no fun never took a political-science course from Knuckles Malone. He came up with a great stunt to use with your two least favorite politicos, especially if they don't like each other.

Knuckles says to take apart a dozen smoke alarms, being sure you use the type that contains radioactive materials. You can check this by looking for the little sticker that must be placed on all items containing radioactive material.

Use some type of play dough to shape it like plastique around a small metal box containing the radioactive parts of the smoke alarms. Attach wires to a cheap timer and stick the wires into the middle of the clay mass. Run another set of different colored wires from the mass into the metal box, then to the timer again.

You have created an imaginative toy, a non-functioning nuclear bomb. Knuckles says he feels free to send this device, properly wrapped in a box, from one of his political marks to the other. An appropriate card can be included, of course.

He also says you can use some imagination with the box chosen to house the bomb, e.g., choosing a carton to add further gender, religious, or racial slurs to the bomb idea.

In addition to reminding you of the usual rules for Hayduke security, Knuckles adds that you need to wear protective clothing when handling the radioactive parts from the smoke alarms, "just to be on the safe side," as he puts it.

He also reminds us, quite unnecessarily, that a lot of people will view this stunt with no sense of humor at all. You can usually spot these types because the expression of their faces resembles a smoker's collapsed lung.

OFFICE

That fun old son of a buck, Tired Of Them, shared a great way of getting back at officious bosses and other jerks in the workplace. Tired used to work for a guy whose lips seemed to be permanently sealed to some higher-up's ass. The jerk was rarely at his desk, as he was usually off kissing ass.

You know the type: seven-year-old puckered pants, reject-shop necktie, and a decade-old blazer with stitching flaws, making it look as if it's been strafed with bug shit. This guy also owns a leisure suit he's keeping for a comeback. His mother looks like Tony Galento coming off a ten-day drunk.

Because he was never at his desk, the staff used to have to take his phone messages for him. As payback, they started giving him maybe 20 percent of them daily. The rest they put in a folder, which they hid in a file drawer of his that they marked PERSONAL: STAY OUT! This was a secure area because he rarely did any real work there.

After three weeks of Kingass Bozo missing meetings and deadlines and not returning calls, his boss called him in for a conference. While this was going on, another boss looked through the man's files. Guess what he found.

The Asskisser had no excuse or explanation. He also had no future with this company and soon moved on. Hee hee, the wages of this sort of sin are far above union scale. Thus, in this sort of memo war—verbal or otherwise—it pays to read between the lions.

◆

Another fun stunt suggested by Biggus Piraphicus is to mess with your office mark's Rolodex. You can switch entire files, remove files, change numbers, interchange names and numbers, or even insert new names and numbers. I can think of many very amusing specifics here.

PARTY

A friend stiffs you, cheats on or with you, or somehow upsets you a tad. It's no biggie, but some frantic fun is in order. Weird Wes has a suggestion.

Wes says it's better if your intended mark is someone who makes frequent trips out of town. Also, you need to know the dates of anniversary or birthday celebrations for this mark. Sometimes these appear in local newspapers.

Wes says to purchase some truly sleazy/sexy bimbo lingerie, such as skimpy, crotchless panties. Have them gift-wrapped after spraying on some heavy-musk cheap perfume and adding a sexually graphic card.

Have the parcel, with more perfume spray, delivered on the day of the event. Naturally, the card has some sentiment expressed on it, usually of a carnal nature. Let's hope, as Wes does, that the mark's spouse, sweetie, or whoever is ill-amused by all of this. By the way, it doesn't matter whose gender is which in this scenario.

◆

The Alaskan had an acquaintance who was especially obnoxious as a party guest. As a British friend of mine once remarked about this sort of dastardly chap, "He vomited so often you could skate home on the sick." The Alaskan was bound to get even.

Turning to the local newspaper for help, he obtained a huge stack of unusable papers from their pressroom. The Alaskan brought them to the next party at the acquaintance's apartment.

"Several of us waited until such time as he passed out. We turned his bed around to disorient him, removed all of his light bulbs, then tripped the circuit breakers for his bedroom, hall, and bathroom. We then crumpled up all of this newspaper and packed it around him and the room," The Alaskan reports.

He says it took them two hours to fill enough of the room to panic the drunk when he awoke, yet leave him air. The Alaskan says he never heard a word about this from the drunk himself. However, another friend stayed in the living room until he heard the drunk stirring in the early morning. The others had, of course, drawn all the shades.

"There was much crashing, trashing, screaming—almost in terror—then cursing, with more loud bumps," The Alaskan recounts, adding that their accomplice left the apartment at this point.

PETS

Normally, dogs don't know as much as humans, which is why they make such good companions and friends. Show dogs, however, tend to be snotty extensions of their masters. Such was the experience of Riam, a wonderful Left Coast lady, who was double-crossed, lied to, and finally cheated out of a good friendship by a bitch of the human sort.

"I wanted to get to that woman and figured two ways were through her dogs and her purse. I didn't want to hurt the dogs—it wasn't their fault they had to share life with this two-legged shrew. So, I did some serious thinking," Riam explained.

Riam settled on a small garden sprayer and a supply of long-lasting hair dye in a variety of punker colors. While the madam of the dogs was away one evening, Riam went quietly to her home and coaxed the four dogs to the fence.

"I spray-colored each dog an outrageous neon/punk hue. It didn't hurt them in the least. They thought it was a game. I mean, what do they care what color they are?"

She said that it was three months before Mrs. Bowwow was able to show her prize dogs. She lost ring time and prize money. And the neighbor kids thought it was a gas . . . they loved the punk-rocker pups.

It's too bad Ed Sullivan and his *bigggggg shooouuuu* are no longer with us. However, there is David Letterman and his stupid pet-owner tricks.

◆

Sr. ForGool had a problem with the neighbors' dogs dumping on his lawn. He also has a solution. At night, he feeds the mark's dog cheap hamburger laden with laxative. Then, using one of those silent dog whistles, ForGool says to use the single-tone type, not the adjustable model, blow a long, steady blast to signal the dog to bark.

When the owner comes out to yell at his dog, stop the whistle's signal. When the owner leaves, blow again. The idea is to keep this pattern up until the owner allows the dog in the house.

Surely, you can figure out the rest of this yourself. Let's hope the mark allows this dog to sleep in the same room as he or she. One good dump deserves another and another and another.

Speaking of offal joy, unless you enjoy fumigating your house, never feed a large dog egg salad. If I have to explain why, you need to have the experience. Once; right, Rusty?

PHOTOGRAPHY

Old George Eastman, founder of Kodak, used to say, "You push the button, we'll do the rest." I have found someone with a delightful sense of humor who has modified Mr. Eastman's slogan significantly. I refer to Magic Z.

To pull off his stunt, you need access to your mark's camera and a bunch of raunchy porno pictures, in color, of course. Your first step is to use your camera to copy the pornopix onto a roll of 35mm color film. Rewind just enough film into the cartridge that it still looks new and unused.

Then, if your mark's camera is loaded, replace his blank film with the one you've just shot. Or put your porno-exposed film back into a film canister or box, carefully seal it, and put it with the mark's film supply to be used later.

The idea here is to create a double-exposed roll of nasty pictures that will add interesting results to your unsuspecting mark's innocent shots. Most 35mm films will give great superimposition photos. That way, your mark will get back his own classic shots, hopefully of once-in-a-lifetime vacation or family pictures, and the raunchy porn shots will be superimposed on his.

Magic Z pulled this one on a dork in his school, and the mark got into some serious trouble with the photo-club adviser who thought the kid had been fooling around with porn stuff using a school camera. Great kidder, that Magic Z Man!

PLANTS, GARDENS, & LAWNS

Lawn work is suburban man's life effort to improve his lot. This same lawn, garden, plants, shrubs, and other flora and fauna are also grand targets for an alert trickster, a la old Spike Ellis, a proud cowpuncher who's tossed a few bullies in his day. He says he finds Elanco's tebuthiuron, sold under the tradename of Spike (hmmmm?), is a real nasty destroyer of plants and other growing things.

"The company's literature lists three pages of species that this stuff will quickly and permanently murder. It's a no-nonsense herbicide designed for terminal brush control," our Texas pal reports.

Once again, technology comes to the aid of the frustrated Hayduker. Better fun through chemistry, eh gang? By the way, I tried some on an experimental basis, and it does the job. It's innocently available at gardening shops everywhere.

◆

I guess this next bit of horrendous horticultural information is properly reported in this section. Thank Anna Spathe for this useful information, regardless of where you found it and how well you use it. I have and did; it works well.

Crown of India, as it's known in layperson's terms, is an unusual plant that stands two to three feet tall and flowers in late winter or early spring. So what, you say? Stick with me. In a short time, the entire plant begins to smell like carrion. Now do you see why Anna and I have introduced you to Crown of India?

As Anna puts it, perhaps more delicately as befits her nature, "The damn thing reeks like the crotch of a motorcycle mamma's panties after a two-week summer run without a change."

Anna says she once left several of these fine plants in a relative's basement over the winter, "just for a few laughs." She says the folks nearly tore the basement apart trying to find a decaying, dead animal that "had to be there, it smelled so bad."

You're now on your own.

POLICE

Unhappily, many police officers have to deal with people that most of you don't want to know anything about. I have a cousin who's a cop, and being with him on the job is scary. There are a lot of really evil things out there.

Scuzzbuster is a former officer who related one of the finer little Haydukerings, as he called it, that he and his partner used to perform on the truly deserving of the penis-drippings (a.k.a. street slime and criminals) they had to arrest.

"We saved this for the truly nasty, violent animals, the bullies who beat up and robbed kids and old ladies, scum like that," Scuzzbuster recalled. "We'd cuff 'em and put them in the back of the car but 'forget' to fasten their seatbelts. We'd be on our way to the lockup at about 60 MPH when, gee, we thought a dog had run in front of the car, so I'd slam on the brakes *hard!*"

Scuzzbuster says that the bad guys in the back would hit the cage front at about 25 MPH, usually face first. He says he would also rock the car around corners to bang the jerks together if there were a couple of suspects back there, or just into the sides of the vehicle if there was one guy. You have no bracing protection when you're cuffed with your hands behind you. His favorite stunt was slamming the brakes so the cruds' faces would hit the screen.

"We called this game Waffleface. If they bled, we'd call it Waffleface and Syrup."

I admire that man's sense of devotion to duty almost as much as his sense of humor.

◆

Speaking of a sense of humor, Roadshow Phil from New Mexico nominates the Immigration and Naturalization Service (INS), a busy bureau of the U.S. Department of Just Us, for a Big Snort Laugh Award. The INS is, of course, the keeper of our nation's borders. As such, they are charged with policing aliens, many of whom are illegal migrant workers. These poor folks do jobs the rest of us won't, and for slave wages and squalid living conditions that our farm animals would report as abusive.

Phil says all of the above may be used for your mark's education. There is an INS form known as I-9 that must be completed for each alien. There is also a follow-up form that employers are required to sign to verify that they have had their workers complete the I-9 forms; or if not, why not.

By now, I am sure the idea is beginning to gleam in your mind. What if someone with a sense of humor completed one of these follow-up verification forms with the mark's name, address, and phone number, telling the INS "*Hell no!*" about cooperation? Add some personal comments about INS and its specific personnel in the mark's regional office, fold, staple, and mail.

It's now out of your hands. The INS will handle the rest for you.

◆

Speaking of which, a few weeks before writing this section, I had some business to attend to in the Honduran Alps, just north of Nicaragua, in a tiny place called Cono Carajo, where I talked to some plainclothes nuns about tricks. Our discussion turned to the new generation of sheep-dipped American advisors who were training the recycled Contras for our government's newest scam, the War on Drugs. We were discussing the Contras' marksmanship.

"Most of 'em couldn't hit Rosanne Barr at two feet," was the terse professional opinion of a shadow warrior I've known for twenty-nine years.

The Big Drug War. There's another diplomatic hand grenade exploded in a honey bucket. But, trust 'em, because they're our police. Yeah, like that old Latin saying, *Quis custodiet ipsos custodes*, which means, who will watch the watchmen?

POOP

Riam told me about this next trick, as did Nightrain, Duke, Sundance, and Liz. I confirmed it with two other bartenders and one pharmacist.

A couple of drops of Visine or other generic eye wash will create a lively day or so of poop and scoop for your mark. Indeed, when he told me about it, Duke said, "When I've used this, I called it the mark's 'see how fast and often I can run to the can' game. Sometimes the mark doesn't make the can, so then the whatever/wherever becomes the dumping ground."

As Sundance, himself a former bartender, noted, "And you thought Visine was good only for getting out the red."

◆

Our little feathered neighbors can be trained to rain their poop on your mark's party, according to veteran trickster, Chester the Spoon. Natural divebombers and mostly territorial, birds can be fed, says Chester, in an area around your mark's targeted possession.

"If you feed the birds, nature will arm them, and their instinct will take care of the rest," Chester reports. "I could tell you many stories of us using birds and their poop to repay many disfavors with many targets, including swimming pools, new cars, patios, solar panels, washlines, hee, hee, hee..."

Chester was unable to finish his explanation.

◆

As proof that a fireman is someone who will knock on your front door with an ax, Hoze from Oregon's Portland wrote to tell me how he and some fellows had a few yuks with a very stuffy fire department captain who used to model his caring behavior for his fire fighters on the same sensitive nature of Maj. Frank Burns of *M*A*S*H* infame.

"When it came to dealing with others this guy was a real shithead," Hoze noted. "So, we helped him live up to that."

It seems that Capt. Shithead had a private crapper that he insisted be kept spotless by the fireman of his command. He also insisted that it not be used by these mere mortals.

Hoze said they started out slowly, then escalated the fun. Here are a few of the quick steps along their path to payback for this pompous poopy prick.

• On Sunday morning, shortly before Capt. Shithead was due into his private domain, two or three of the guys who'd eaten hard-boiled eggs, cabbage, and other goodies, washed down by flagons of strong ale, would take an unflushed dump in his prestigious private privy. Nobody flushed. This was repeated on staggered days of staggered weeks, always at random times.

- Hoze says the boys hand-rolled some semi-hardened fudge into good-sized dumplings and placed them in a trail from the hated officer's desk to his dumper. Moments before, some volunteers had filled the dumper with the real thing.
- In a similar scenario, Hoze says that fudge was used, not true dump product, to place smeared handprints all over the potty paper, nearby wall, the captain's desk, telephone, and office door. When this stunt was repeated nearly two months later, one wag did substitute real poo poo to smear a handprint on the desktop photo showing the captain posed with the mayor.

As a word to those who've been worrying about fingerprints left by the handsmears instead of laughing along with the rest of us, rest assured that Hoze had the guys wear rubber gloves.

What happened? There were roll-call lectures, internal investigations, and finally the police were called in. Nobody laughed, cracked, or even reacted. But, Hoze says they just kept up the pressure. The captain finally took a transfer after ten months.

Flushed with success, the men held a large party.

♦

J.J. of Boston tells me that a few tablespoons of baking soda in a pot of freshly brewed coffee will have your mark's ass on the porcelain throne for hours. He notes that adding about a teaspoon to a cup of coffee gets the same results.

According to J.J., the trick is to tell your mark, "Gee, it must be something you ate or a virus. Better drink some coffee to fight back."

♦

Gen and Bert saw this and thought what a wonderful thing it would be to send a similar message to their least favorite supervisor from their days working at an amusement park. Did they? Ask Uncle Gerry and Rusty, who swear this actually happened. I checked it out with Anton Putzela, who was at the same family reunion, and he also swears it's true . . . good enough for me. Here's what happened.

Uncle Gerry had to create one of his famous islands in the porcelain pool. So, he goes into the bog at the reunion site and notices this sign above the crapper, which reads: PLEASE DO NOT PUT ANYTHING IN THIS TOILET BOWL BUT TOILET PAPER. So, being the truly obedient guy he is, Uncle Gerry takes his dump on the floor, puts the toilet paper in the can, flushes it away, and walks out.

PORNO

We were sitting around the bishop's study at the Church of the Lantern-day Saints in greater downtown Salmon discussing the meeting the Sisters of Sappho had the other evening at Burl Yates High School. Lyle Gorch brought up the name of Mike R. from L.A., one of the more twisted revengers in action today.

"Speaking of schools, Mike did some creative editing on some dippy, feel-good-about-our-drug-free-kids movie the PTA was showing at Edwin Meese Memorial High School over in East L.A. He managed to get the print and exchanged parts of it for little snatches of frames from 'Debbie Does Dallas,' some of Seka's movies, and others," Lyle explained.

"Naturally, he used snippets of cum shots, getting and giving head, some gay-guy stuff. So, when the audience saw the film, they'd get the normal PTA stuff, then about a second of porn, with several minutes of PTA, then another second of porn. It was kind of like subliminal seduction. I guess some people really got pissed off," Lyle added.

The Bishop blessed Mike R. from L.A. right on the spot. We all then belched in agreement.

Mike later told me that he once edited in a thirty-second shot of a couple fornicating just after the narrator on a school historical film asked, "And, just why is George Washington known as the father of our country?" The kids in the class went nuts with laughter while the teacher nearly had a stroke.

◆

The Alaskan had a pious, nosy college roommate. This kid was a member of the White Ribbon Commandos, those religious assholes with white ribbons on their car antennas who are always trying to get *Playboy* banned from the local convenience store. The Alaskan tried to live his own life and ignore this Bible-thumping bigot, but to no avail.

"While he was out mentally beating off somewhere at some meeting of Citizens for Decency in Thought and Mind, I got a truly porno centerfold from some nasty magazine. I taped it on the outside of the window on this guy's side of the room. Now, this was brutal cold winter in northern Ohio, so ice is only a breath away," The Alaskan recalled.

Slowly and carefully, our hero sprayed water from a spritzer bottle on the poster until ice formed. He kept this up until there was three-quarters of an inch of hard, clear ice covering the picture and the window.

"We were across from the main walkway and the administration building, so you can imagine the hassle this caused. There were many complaints, but as I had left for home for the weekend before my asshole roomie got back . . ."

The Alaskan said it took the mark over an hour to remove the poster, and he cracked the window. Our hero denied any knowledge of the trick, and, as he'd been signed out to be home, he was not implicated. An unidentified prowler was blamed, and the religious asshole had to pay for the window.

That's as it should be.

◆

Remember Anonymous from a few books ago? She's back with a fun stunt intended to pay back an evil, gossipy old monster for whom she worked a few years ago. She says the old cretin was a hardcore puritan, which is where she got this grand idea.

"I learned that he belonged to a regional poetry club, comprised of blue/white-haired little old ladies, retiring English teachers, effete professors (are there any other sort?), and a few serious poets," she told me.

"One of their activities was to send each other their poetry, mailing photocopies in a sort of mass mailing, a kind of chain mail of literari, I guess. I'm sure you can predict what I did."

Indeed, Anonymous cleverly crafted a lovely poem dripping with adoring, young chickenhawk love all the gay way. Here is a sample of her poetry:

Your touch of tight ass may give me a surge
But it's little blonde boys who give me the urge.

Pulling undies off of peach-fuzzy butts
Bulges my pants and tickles my nuts.

I'm certain you get the drift of that message. Next, through a friend, Anonymous got the poetry group's mailing list. Being very, very careful, she prepared this poem as if by her mark, made multiple copies, then mailed one to each member of the group from the mark.

Two days later, she sent a copy of a copy, again being very careful, to the city police department's vice squad and a copy to the youth-services people in the courthouse. She explained that she was a poetry-club member, wishing to remain anonymous, who was merely doing her civic duty.

◆

Once there was this really grumpy old lady who left her car at a national car-care franchise outlet at which George from USCG used to work. She was a nasty piece of work, always complaining, plus she smelled like a zookeeper's shoe. So George had some fun.

"This mean old hag brought her car in twice a month with imaginary ailments and problems. She always paid her bills, but she was a time-taking royal pain in the ass.

"One time when she brought in her car, she left her camera on the backseat. As the car had to stay overnight, I borrowed the camera and took it home with me.

"My girlfriend, Vanna Cherry, was over for the night, and we decided to goof around with the camera. She took a picture of my hard dick, and I took a couple of her lack of dick. I put the camera back in the old broad's car."

George says he never heard a word about the incident, but that the old lady missed bringing in her car for more than six weeks. I figure that it may have taken that long for her vibrator's batteries to die, George.

◆

Speaking of toys for twats, Dick Smegma offers a stunt that was used to correct the nasty activities of someone who had successfully evaded the law because of political connections. A lady bought a ten-inch, black dildo, complete with anatomically correct detail, of course, then wrapped it very nicely with a special card "signed" by her mark. The card read, "The sooner you get started practicing with this, my little darling sweetie, the sooner you'll be ready to take me on." The gift was wrapped in pink paper imprinted with little bears and other cute stuff.

To whom did this gift go? It was addressed to a little neighbor girl who lived near the mark, but it was delivered in such a way that her parents would obviously see it and open it before if got to their daughter. Dick leaves the resultant action against the mark to your imagination, except to add, "My, oh my, twat fun!"

POSTERS

Dick Smegma calls this one "Aiming for the Eyes." There was a disgusting politician—whoa, isn't that redundant? Anyway, one of Dick's friends had six hundred waterproof posters printed with a large picture of his mark, a local politician, with the phrase AIM FOR HIS EYES in large type across the politician's forehead.

Dick says his pal went into high-volume public men's rooms, dried off the urinal walls, and stuck these adhesive-back posters on the back of the urinals. Thus, when guys came in to take a leak, they had a target. Oh well, it's almost as good as the real thing.

Your mark for this doesn't have to be an elected thing. It could be an ex-sweetie, a neighbor, a boss, or just about anyone whose face you would enjoy pissing upon.

In a similar situation, the Giant Panda suggested gluing a waterproofed photo/poster of your mark on the toilet seat, either top or bottom. Perhaps the slogan SIT ON MY FACE would have some special meaning here.

QUOTES

As I do in each of my books, I am including wonderfully fine and funny quotes that are available for you to use in your life.

These quotes make fine philosophy for your own peace of mind, are creative thoughts to muse upon, or can be used as graffiti or custom bumper stickers. They also make great lines to spice your conversation.

"Men who sleep well at night will march better in the morning."
—Mao Tse-tung

"Criticism by assholes is a good sign that you're doing something right."
—Jeff Salzman

"Money, not morality, is the principal commerce of civilized nations."
—Thomas Jefferson

"You can kill ten of my men for every one I kill of yours. But, even at those odds, you will lose and I will win."

—Ho Chi Minh

"I laugh and my laughter is not within me; I burn and the burning is not seen outside."

—Niccolo Machiavelli

"You lie, you die, simple as that."

—Moolinyahms

"The first time I saw George McGeary, I thought he was the doorman at the Nogales jail's drunk tank."

—Lyle Gorch

"A kind word and a gun will get you farther than just a kind word."

—Al Capone

"When the best leader's work is done, the people say, 'We did it ourselves.'"

—Lao-Tzu

"In war there is no second prize for runner-up."

—Omar Bradley

"He who lives by the sword sometimes gets it stuck up his ass."

—George McGeary

"The reasonable man adapts himself to the world; the unreasonable man persists in trying to adapt the world to himself. Therefore, all progress depends upon the unreasonable man."
—George Bernard Shaw

"You do not make an omelet without first breaking some eggs."
—Midden Loecher

"The printer . . . without him tyrants and humbugs in all countries would have their own way. He is a friend of intelligence and thought."
—Charles Dickens

"Never interrupt an enemy while he's making a mistake."
—Napoleon Bonaparte

"Holy shit and three thunders!"
—Rev. Burundanga Du Ma

Rev. Nastyman has gone through some educational experiences with the American judicial system. Considering my feelings about the U.S. Just Us Department, I've enjoyed the more quotable parts of Rev. Nastyman's letters. Here are some of his gems about our legal system.

"Bullshit is always edible in the press and in law."

"The way to win in court is to have either more bullshit, more money, or both."

"More cases are decided between urinals than between jurors."

"What do you mean you don't trust us, we're police officers."

Another person who has some experience with the American legal system is Robert Vesco, great friend of you know which former American president. These are his immortal words.

"The only way to emerge victorious in courtroom litigation is a commitment to honesty, integrity, and justice." Ha, ha, ha, ha, ha, ha. Whoooo!! Ho, ho, ho. Ha hah!

RADAR

It's really great to get technical support from my readers, and as some are good, honest police officers, I get the straight stuff from them. Thanks to Scuzzbuster, you now have some solid technical advice about how to use radar for your benefit and not that of the officer who's using it on you.

Most police radar units have an electronic device known as a radio frequency interference indicator (RFI) that blanks out the radar gun's speed display window whenever there is any type of electromagnetic voltage interference. This is to protect the unit's sensitive electronics from burnout. Thus, when the RFI kicks on, the unit will not display any reading.

According to Scuzzbuster, simply keying the mike on your mobile CB in the proximity of a radar gun will kick on the RFI and render the gun useless. The limit on distance is about one-quarter of a mile, unless, of course, you have one of those illegal boosters known as a linear amplifier (see CB). That might get you out to a mile or mile and a half. Scuzzbuster says a two-hundred-watt "kicker" should give you all that you need.

Scuzzbuster also says that modern radar guns can easily defeat radar detectors. In fact, he calls most detectors "useless, bullshit rip-offs." He says the current radar guns have a "hold/mode" button, or "instant on," which turns the radar on and off with a reading so fast your detector might not even beep.

"You're far better off jamming radar than you are detecting it," Scuzzbuster says. "If you're in an area with radar, simply find an open, unused channel on your CB, then tape down the transmit button on your mike. You're jamming radar guns within a mile or so of you."

If all of this weren't being done in fun and not for actual use, I'd be tempted to warn you not to get caught jamming radar. Under the new federal emergency guidelines, that calls for summary roadside execution.

RADICALS

As I grow older, I grow more radical in my dislike for other things radical. For example, radical Republican rightists ought to be vulcanized into radial tires. Radical leftist whatevers could be strained into semiorganic fertilizer. Or, as that magnificent philosopher Amarante Cordova said of some greedy, radical, capitalist land developers one day, "A large wolf will eat you and shit you out as a wet, green puddle."

Barney Vincelette's least favorite radicals are the truly fringe-end feminists who want to decojone any and all males. I share his view, except that I am really frightened by some of these alleged females, many of whom usually are dressed like animated garage sales and have a personality that needs a volume control.

A creative chap, Barney has modified my suggestion for using your 35mm camera and some imagination to create personal message postal cards. Barney has posed a young lady in a waist to head shot, dressed in a Nazi uniform and Hitler mask. She's pulling open her blouse to flash us, and that's how we know she's female.

The message written on the face of this card, printed above and below the model, says "I COULDN'T HELP THE HOLOCAUST. PMS MADE ME DO IT."

He sends these cards to radical persons who piss him off.

ROADKILL

You'd best sit down to read this one. It has the potential to be one of the most impactful stunts I have ever reported. It rivals the special effects of Hollywood's finest and, in its simplicity and terror, the work of a true mind terrorist. The diabolical diviner of this devilish debacle is Terminator X. Here is his tale.

He says that roadkilled variety is OK, but something fresher and less flattened is better. Terminator X adds, "If it's available, I prefer a freshly dead cat with no puncture wounds, as you'll soon note why."

The equipment needed includes a gallon of gasoline, a flexible tube (e.g., a small-diameter garden hose), a funnel, twine, and a long, woolen sock.

Curious? Paw forward a bit, then, and maybe you'll find some of this amewsing.

You may wish to drain the cat of whatever fluid it still has, then *jam* the piece of hose down its throat until it plunks into the lung and stomach cavity. Come on, folks, lighten up.

172

What the hell, it's dead!

Next, attach the funnel to the garden hose and carefully and slowly pour the gasoline down the tube. This will take some time as the body, still fresh, has to absorb the gasoline. Obviously, you want to keep the cat upright at all times. When the body is filled, remove the tube and cover it with the sock. Then, jam the sock-covered tube back down the deceased's throat.

You have now inserted the fuze for what Terminator X calls his Exploding Pussy Prank. The next step is to remove the rubber tube while making certain that the sock stays down the throat. Wrap the twine very tightly around the cat's throat and pull tight before tying it off. You don't want any of the gasoline to leak out.

As part of your planning for this trick, you should have devised a means of rapid and covert departure. At the target area, quickly soak the protruding end of the sock with lighter fluid so you get a burning, not an exploding, fuze. Place the feline pyrotechnic in position, light the fuze, and *rapidly* depart the impact area.

Terminator X used this stunt once to make his point with an old friend who'd been ripping off his property. He noted, "I knocked on the guy's door, lighted the fuze, and split. The cat will explode raw, smelly mess everywhere, or it will burn as a very terrible pyre. Either way, it makes a helluva impact. In my enemy's case, it exploded and showered him and his porch with mega-disgusting mess."

I agree, it sure is disgusting. So, why are you laughing? I have an excuse, I have no pretensions of civilization.

◆

Another interesting use for fresh roadkill comes from Mahng Tia. For this silly scenario, you need to collect or create some fresh roadkill, hopefully of the domestic pet variety. I trust I do not need to be more specific.

Next, just like an old-time hunter or buffalo skinner, prepare the body as if you were going to cook and feed from it: remove the head, outer skin, glands, and innards and put these in a clear plastic bag. Your next move is to place this large bag in the Dumpster of a restaurant or fast-food outlet that has offended you. Go to the nearest pay telephone and alert the following local outlets: American Society for the Prevention of Cruelty to Animals (ASPCA), Animal Friends, police, health authorities, and news media. Tell them that you are an employee of the mark/restaurant, and you've seen evidence that they serve dog and/or cat meat to patrons. Enjoy.

SCHOOLS

This next idea, which works best around colleges or large high schools, comes from John McGeary's buddy Darren in San Diego. If you've been around many campii, you know that people are always losing stuff or getting it ripped off. Indeed, I suspect there are more thieves on America's campii than there are in the nation's prisons. Darren thinks we can put this fact to good use.

"When you see one of those REWARD FOR RETURN signs put all over campus by people who lose stuff or get ripped off, call the person," Darren says. "Tell them you're the one who stole the whatever and that you're not giving it back."

Darren says to add to the hassle by insulting the quality of the missing item and its owner. If it's a missing stereo, tell the owner that s/he is a cheap, stupid bastard and to get a good one next time, one that plays CDs.

"If they scream back and argue, so much the better. Insult them more. Try to learn ethnic info about them, or their hometown, sorority or fraternity, whatever, and use it against them. Tell 'em you're coming by again and to have some good stuff for you to steal," Darren adds.

It might be fun to make this call from a school office or a teacher's office, in hopes the call is being traced. Otherwise, use a pay phone and leave the area fast after hanging up.

◆

There are a lot of laughs going around Oak Ridge High in El Dorado Hills, California, not the least of which are being caused by truly amusing people performing justice upon truly deserving marks.

Another Darren trick is to smear Vaseline carefully on critical floor areas in your school, i.e., outside of administrators' or coaches' offices, teacher bathrooms, or elsewhere. Vaseline also works well in the earpieces of school telephones, especially in administrative, coaches', or teachers' offices. If I may add one caveat, do these things only to *prick* teachers. It's been my experience as a scholastic student and athlete that most administrators and coaches are already pricks, so don't worry about doing nasty shit to them.

◆

When Misfit was a Brooklyn high-school student, he knew a particular student who used to asskiss his way to everything. This reminds me of a young lady I once knew, a frieze-dried office gossip who used to follow her boss around so closely that if he'd made a sharp turn, her nose would have been broken. In Misfit's case, the crime was the same, the gender different. And, he used that.

Six weeks before graduation, he had a female friend call the mark's parents during school hours. In a small, scared voice she asked if the young man was home. Of course not, he was in school. She left the teary message to "Tell him Mary called and it's real important!"

The mark had no idea about the call and shrugged it off. Four weeks later, on purloined school letterhead, Misfit sent a letter to Mark's folks to advise them that their son apparently had impregnated a thirteen-year-old eighth grader named Mary. I am sure you follow what happened. The letter said to contact the principal as soon as possible.

Misfit mailed it on a Friday, so the parents had it all weekend. In addition, their son, the young mark, was away that weekend, and the principal had an unlisted number. So, the old folks got to stew over it until late Sunday evening. To make matters more fun, Misfit had his lady friend call again Sunday to tearfully ask the parents for young mark. When they attempted to talk to her she began to wail and hung up.

The point is, who cares what happened Monday or Tuesday? Think about the mistrust and paranoia all around.

◆

I'm not sure to whom the thanks rolls out for this one, either Jamie from radio station KTAR or

Dave from Arizona State University. Either way, it's from the Valley of the Sun, and it seems to be a whole lotta shaking fun going on.

It seems the Frat Boys held this really fun party, which seems somewhat oxymoronic, but let's not ruin the story before we begin. Only one thing marred the fun party and that is that the promised-to-be-there Sorority Sisters didn't show up as promised. There was mega-embarrassment for the gods of frat: their women had stood them up in front of guests.

The Frat Boys were truly insulted. Their women hadn't shown up to make the scene, which is a macho/property thing, I suspect. But, to prove there were no hard feelings, the frat guys sent two dozen doughnuts over to the girls at their sorority suite the following Sunday morning. A nice touch, eh?

Later, that same afternoon, a fraternity pledge showed up at the sorority suite and posted on their bulletin board two large, glossy five-by-seven enlargements showing a group of the better-hung frat boys wearing doughnuts on portions of their anatomy. A brief note said, "So good of you to take part in the postgame ceremonies from our ring toss this morning."

Sure, it's a childish stunt. Sure it's crude. It's also funny, and, most happily, it is a true story. Nothing quite like tossing it off, then, is there?

◆

Speaking of true stories, Bryan "The Butcher" Fear, a one-time living legend at Mt. Carmel, got into deep trouble with school Hitler wannabes for being a truthful wiseass. He wrote a series of letters to the school newspaper in which he shouted out about real problems these same ineffectual administrators, a redundancy, could not curb. He used clever turn of phrase and truth to make his point and to infuriate them. A sample follows:

Dear Editor,
I am a Mt. Carmel senior who has a serious problem. It involves alcohol, tobacco, drugs, sex, suicide, disease, and serious traffic accidents and vehicle abuse. My problem is that I have nothing to do with any of these. Do you realize what a tiny, tiny percentage of living students that leaves me in?

The letter continued, emphasizing how poorly the administrators administered the school, despite their public relations to the contrary. It was beautiful, tongue-in-their-ear work.

◆

As we head toward a new century, why does it seem that education grows lesser? For my own purposes, I attended a meeting recently of educational administrators and those professors who teach new teachers. All of it reminded me of the colorless cell-splitting in the bland end of the gene pool. I think Bart Simpson may be correct.

SEWAGE

Ahh, alas, The Skull is back, married, and just as full of fun as ever. He tells me he's finally gotten his dream, a camper for himself and his bride to tour the country. It comes equipped with a ready-made Hayduking idea. Let The Skull explain.

"This big old camper has a twenty-five-gallon holding tank for what they euphemistically call 'gray water' from our little mobile sewer system. Never one to waste anything, I have made grand use of it," says The Skull.

One of the bullies he dumped on was his new bride's ex. She left the guy because he was a violent, nasty asshole. And, true to form, the asswipe caused her all sorts of trouble, up to and including her marriage to The Skull, who was not part of their breakup.

"This swine won't take polite reasoning, and he's too dumb to hurt, so I've been having a lot of laughs. I use a little, portable holding tank into which I empty our camper's main sewage taps. While he was away on vacation for a week, I took several loads of this stuff over to his place and sprayed it all over his lawn, shrubs, and patio.

"He may not be able to attract human friends, but he sure was doing great with insects and rodents. His neighbors were furious at him, with no idea how the, literally, crap had gotten there," The Skull reported.

For a kicker, on the day the ex was due home, Mrs. Skull called the city, county, and state health authorities to "officially" complain about this sewage dump at the ex's place. She claimed to be from the mayor's office, which got faster service. Her ex was forced to dig up his septic tank and all lines to find "the leak."

The Skull reports that after all of this calms down, he plans to start making more nocturnal deliveries of slop, adding, "The fool never locks his expensive foreign sports car. Does that give me any target ideas?"

◆

When it comes to natural methods of destroying septic systems, Zero Man has a couple of ideas—one of which is to flush several packs of cigarettes down the toilet of your mark's home septic system.

"The tobacco in those ciggies will kill most of the bacteria in the septic tank, thus destroying the operating field," says Zero Man. "That means if you do it several times a day, you will soon have this mark standing ankle deep in backed-up shit."

Cigarettes are a good choice. Or, you can also

flush a gallon or so of laundry bleach down the toilet as well. But, how innocent would you look carrying a gallon of bleach versus three packs of cigarettes to a party at the mark's place?

SEX

Clifford Odets defined sex as poor man's polo. Meantime, XXMagic used this lowest common denominator of human lust to get back at a mark who had nearly destroyed his family by stealing his wife away from him and their kids. What XXMagic did was to list the mark with two or three X-rated computer dating services.

These services generally use the "976" telephone networks to take the initial call. Then, you make payment arrangements via credit card, and you are then given another number to call. You are now in the system.

At this point, XXMagic gave some hilariously detailed sexual-preference disinformation about his mark, the man who'd taken away his wife. He listed the sap with two services, once as a passive gay into bondage and once as a studly heterosexual with large equipment and strong needs.

Our hero had access to the mark's phone number and credit information, which he used well at good old 976 (see In Privity to learn how to gather the necessary personal information on your mark). Within three weeks, his distraught and by now ex-wife told XXMagic about this "secret life" her boyfriend must have been leading and how they had the phone number changed to "stop these awful calls . . . He must have lied to me . . . Oh, what have I ever done?"

XXMagic waited a couple of weeks and did it all again, using the new phone numbers.

◆

Our next stunt comes from super Dick Smegma, who tells me this is supposedly a true story about revenge on a rapist.

A woman drove up to a small motel in a tiny New Mexico town, which had been the scene of three unsolved, violent rapes. Local police were without a clue as to the rapist's identity or how to stop the attacks. The tall, leggy brunette looked as if she were a high-fashion model.

As she approached the front desk, the registration clerk was instantly captivated by her looks. He told her that rooms were available, but politely warned her that three females had been raped in this motel. "Perhaps for your own safety, you might wish to stay elsewhere."

The woman threw back her head and laughed. "I'm not going to let *any* man determine where *I* sleep," she said. "I'm sleeping at *this* motel, and to show you that I'm not afraid, I'm going to leave the door to my room *unlocked*." With that, she signed the guest register as L.A. Jones, picked up her room key and suitcase, and headed for her room. The desk clerk offered to carry her suitcase, but she resisted his gesture, saying, "I carry my own bags. Thank you anyway."

About 6:00 that evening, she ate at the local diner. By 6:45 she had returned to her room to watch television. At 9:00, she called the front desk and told the clerk, "I'm taking a sleeping pill, so I can sleep soundly. If there's a fire or something, please come and get me. As I sleep so soundly, I probably won't hear this phone ringing. As I told you earlier, I'm keeping my door unlocked."

About eleven o'clock that night, a male hand slowly turned the knob on her door. The door was indeed unlocked. The intruder entered the room and spied his victim, as expected, asleep in the bed. Tiptoeing quietly, the attacker crept slowly toward her bed, images flashing in his mind about the violence to follow.

SNAP! A noise, followed by a pain so excruciating the intruder screamed in agony and clutched his right leg, discovering it was soaked in blood. SNAP! SNAP! Two more noises and his other leg and right arm began bleeding profusely from severed arteries in his left thigh and right forearm. His screams of pain, louder than any telephone, awakened his intended victim, who switched on her bedside lamp. There, writhing in torture on the floor, lay the rapist, surrounded by no less than sixteen bear traps, which she had set before retiring.

L.A. Jones rose from her bed, already fully dressed, walked over to the rapist, kicked him in the face, and said, "Take that, snailshit!" His screams followed her out the door and to her car. Ten miles outside of town, she stopped at a pay phone to call the local police. "You'll find that asswipe rapist waiting for you in Room 10 at the Sleepy Hollow Motel on Route 6," she said.

"Who's calling?"

"L.A. Jones, the gal who put him out of business."

"What's the L.A. stand for, Miss?"

"Lady Avenger."

Phew, I remember when sex was all the innocence of drive-ins and dry humps. Today, kids start so young that the prize in a box of Cracker Jack is a condom or a diaphragm. But, surely the makers of the Pill don't yet have it out in the cutesy form of Ninja Turtle characters.

SKATEBOARDERS

I haven't heard much from skateboarders, although I hear a lot about them from their victims or those who have had close traffic calls of the pants-filling variety with them. My young friend Deer, who is a skateboarder, tells me that many of his boarder buddies can't write, so don't.

Deer tells me that one way people have gotten revenge on skateboarders who have hassled them is to infest their paths. Deer says, "Like, it is very nasty to put a bunch of large-caliber rifle ammunition primers in the path of skaters. The boards hit those primers, which explode really loud."

He's right. A skater going over and detonating some of those ammunition primers is likely to be very upset, even off his/her board. Sporting goods shops carry primers.

Deer also suggests scattering small upholsterer's tacks on the skateboarders' path, walk, or wherever they are hassling you.

Otherwise, leave these kids the hell alone. Just because someone's life-style and/or recreational activities differ from yours is no reason to hassle people. Also, hassling them puts you on the other side of the battle, i.e., you become the bully. Don't be a bully.

SMOKERS

Over my years in this fun game, I have offered all sorts of ideas to deal with human smudgepots who pollute the rest of us with their shit-stinky smoke. I thought I'd covered them all, yet, here comes The Knight with a new idea, suggesting that you nip the head off a strike-anywhere match and neatly plant it in your mark's cigarette, cigar, or pipe bowl.

I had the same idea on a larger scale, but haven't figured out yet how to hide a quarter stick of dynamite in those somewhat limited locations.

◆

Another antismoking activist, Uncle Chris, finalized one of his college roommates by gamely collecting the bulk and detritus of ashtray and other tobacco by-products from several bars for a month. He kept this awful heap in several sealed plastic garbage bags.

"I had arranged for an unidentified accomplice to help me," Uncle Chris said. "I was going home for the weekend, and I made sure the mark was in his room and saw me leave. That night, while he was out getting falling down drunk, I had my accomplice come in and seed roomie/smoker's bedroom with the contents of the garbage bags."

An amazing thing happened, Uncle Chris reported. The room was cleaned up by Sunday night, and the kid stopped smoking in their house and moved the next semester.

SOURCES

Following are some annotated sources for materials, ideas, products, and persons that have proven to be helpful in the payback business. This is not a universe of sources, but merely a sampling provided by my experiences, the experiences of others, plus reputation among experts. My listing these sources does not constitute a Good Hayduking Seal of Approval; these are not endorsements or advertisements. Each listing was current at the time of publication.

However, as some companies move, go out of business, or stop communicating with the public, it is possible that you might not get what you want from these listings. You may not even hear back from them. My apologies. In the past, though, the folks I have listed have proven to be excellent sources. If any of you have sources of your own that you'd like to share with the rest of us, drop me a note: George Hayduke, P.O. Box 1307, Boulder, CO 80306.

Allied Publications
Drawer 5070
Glendale, AZ 85312

They list dozens of survival books and manuals that will have definite interest for you. They also sell maps of all sorts and descriptions. Some of their titles will frighten the grown-ups.

Anatomical Chart Company
8221 Kimball
Skokie, IL 60076

I was told this company supplies medical schools and students with charts and other anatomical products. I got one of their catalogs. It can easily supply your needs. If you have the money and a little imagination, you can get a lot of bizarre things from this catalog. Phew!

Black Knight Leathers
205 N. 45th St.
Harrisburg, PA 17111

Here's a great source for all sorts of kinky leather stuff: bondage straps, blinders, meat grinders, and so forth. They sell great stuff for revenge. Also, the owner offers a discount to buyers who mention this book.

Carolina Biological Supply Company
2700 York Road
Burlington, NC 27215

Should you need various insects for your school or other projects—including those large, ugly German cockroaches—these fine folks sell them.

Dallas Delivers
P.O. Box 64566
Dallas, TX 75221

This is a competent and cautious remailing service. I've had contact with the owner and am assured of prompt, private, and very discreet service. The charge is one dollar per letter.

Delta Press, Ltd.
716 Harrell St.
El Dorado, AR 71730

According to my pals in the book industry, these people are one of the most professional, efficient, and easy-to-do-business-with operations selling books these days. Their catalog is colorful, complete, and easy to use. The catalog itself is worth having; it's like a reference bibliography.

The Department of Unconventional Resources
P.O. Box 210352
Columbia, SC 29221

Run by someone called The Wiz, which is slang for Wizard and does not refer to a scatological function, this organization essentially puts into practice that which I put into print. I think they do this only on a harmless and theoretical basis, of course.

Factsheet Five
Mike Gunderloy
6 Arizona Avenue
Rensselaer, NY 12144-4502

Mike Gunderloy is a fine chap who has compiled an excellent, dependable set of references to the underground, independent publishing world. Users tell me each issue repays your modest subscription investment. I have seen and used copies of *Factsheet Five,* an invaluable reference tool to any Hayduker.

Fast Forward Express
P.O. Box 4609
St. Paul, MN 55104

Here are some broad-minded Midwestern folks who will process sexually explicit photos. They are very private, honest, and discreet. Write for brochure.

Jerryco, Inc.
601 Linden Place
Evanston, IL 60202

A gadgeteer's shopping mall between catalog covers best describes these folks. I've bought from them for years, for fun and for fun. They are honest, open, and sell quality goods at very fair prices. Their catalog is written by humans with a sense of humor, a rarity these days.

Johnson Smith Company
4514 19th St. Ct. East
Bradenton, FL 34206-5500

They're back. And so what if they're not in Michigan like when we old duffers were kids. It's still the home of fake vomit, whoopee cushions, dribble glasses, and all the other fun stuff that teachers and mothers hate. They have a lot of other novelty stuff for the '90s, too. My copy sits in the crapper for toilet-time study. Al Bundy told me that he reads his JS catalog there, too.

Loompanics Unlimited
P.O. Box 1197
Port Townsend, WA 98368

This is one of the most useful, fun, and fascinating book businesses around. Michael Hoy is the proprietor and says his book catalog is for knowledge, joy, and pleasure. His catalog is like a library of books, all useful and enjoyable. Michael is a great guy, too. This is my favorite bookshop in the whole world, and that is the truth. Buy from Loompanics! The catalog alone is a magnificent source of rare and highly useful information.

Archie McPhee & Company
Box 30852
Seattle, WA 98103

They advertise remarkable bargains of the most curious sort, and they're very much so. This is one of the most unusual and useful companies with which I do business. Their catalog is a trip in itself, hilarious and informative. For a few bucks, you can stock up enough fun stuff for three years worth of April Fool's days and 150 rainy days. A fun place!

Modern Advisory Institute
P. O. Box 11632
Salt Lake City, UT 84147

Their basic product is a hilarious program called Pranks, which can be installed on your mark's computer or on someone else's computer so your mark gets the credit. Two of the funnier items are Crumble and Insults. Their stuff is relatively harmless but can still create a panic attack or a Maalox moment for your mark.

Photo Kiosk
New London Mall
New London, CT 06320

Here is a trustworthy source for discreet, uncensored photofinishing of your private photos. They do disc and 35mm with twenty-four-hour mail turnaround.

SeXXY Software
Dept 600RV
2800 Bergey Rd.
Hatfield, PA 19440

These guys sell great adult software for your home computer. They have six or seven programs, all great explicit sexual and sensual entertainment. Their SeXXY Disk #1 is a must for Haydukers, and it's not copy-protected, so you can make many copies to use with marks. I've seen their stuff... top rate!

Richard Sitz & Associates
P.O. Box 453
Cedarville, MI 49719

Their major product is a very, very useful report entitled *Telephone Secrets*. This report is filled with information that your local and long-distance telephone companies don't want you to know. For example, it shows you how to legally make Equal Access Codes work for you at no extra cost to you. The report is also a great money saver.

SCO Electronics, Inc.
581 W. Merrick Road
Valley Stream, NY 11580

I don't know these folks, but they did come highly recommended, and I've seen their catalog. They sell outstanding video equipment, including some very nonstandard stuff that Haydukers could use. They also sell other unusual and useful items.

Dick Smegma
P.O. Box 6291
Kahului, HI 96732-6291

This intelligent, experienced, and totally with-it disciple offers personal research services for folks who want to do books, articles, videos, or screenplays about topics germane to this book. His services are available on a commercial consulting basis and are limited to literary efforts.

Square Lake Enterprises
P.O. Box 3673
Logan, UT 84321

I've listed these guys for years, as they are good, honest people to do business with. They sell all sorts of highly useful "special effects" chemicals and other pyrotechnical paraphernalia. They are a good, safe source.

STORES

Jeff Lube and Doc Byte are nice young men who kept getting hassled by store security people who suspected them of loitering, shoplifting, being alive . . . you name it. The irony is that these are bright young men who were legitimate shoppers. It turned out that the security guy had a hard-on for them because he had been a stupid high-school jock who resented anyone whose IQ was above his own negative numbers.

Complaints by these harassed and pissed-off shoppers to the pimple-puss manager—whose head manufactured enough dandruff daily to fill a pillowcase—brought a threat to call the cops.

Our dynamic duo got a clean-cut friend, a twenty-year-old Dan Quayle clone, to go back into the store on a commando raid for them. In the meantime, they had already infiltrated half a dozen other friends for other missions.

It was nothing sophisticated. The main man quietly let himself into the utility room while nobody, including the TV security camera, was watching and turned off all the store's lights.

Being an interior mall store, the place was chaos until the emergency lights came on . . . half of which didn't.

The main man simply blended with other shoppers, while the rest of the crew blundered into things and caused panic. One picked up an "Attention All Fart Shoppers" intercom and said in a BIG voice, "This is God, I have caused a miracle here. Flee this store now or face eternity in hell."

Other people encouraged shoplifting. Several young ladies screamed "*rape!*" over the intercom phone. Then all of the Jeff and Doc commandos simply flowed out with the rest of the terrified shoppers.

◆

Got the small-town-store blues, plus a mark whose chops you want to trash? Storm Trooper has this splendid idea that's highly effective against both marks, provided they know each other, e.g., Mark I is a frequent customer of Mark II's shop. You also need a pay phone outside that store.

Call that pay phone several times a day. It helps if you know the store's busy hours, too. Keep calling until some passing pedestrian answers the phone and then say, "Hello, oh thank God you've answered. Listen, Mark II's (store name) phone line is busy, and this is a real emergency. Would you please run in there and ask for Mr./Ms./Miss/Mrs. Mark I ?"

Put some sincere concern in your voice and

drip with gratitude. Storm Trooper says people will more often than not do this for you. Obviously, doing this several times a day will annoy Mark II. You might also wish to call Mark II's phone number and ask to speak with Mark I.

◆

I was surprised to learn that The Cheshire Cat was angry. He's so calm. Anyway, it seems that his friend had been unfairly fired by a greedhead store manager at the local mall because he thought the kid was giving merchandise to his friends. He wasn't. The irony was, the store manager was.

"I thought things needed to be cleaned up in this store," Cheshire told me. I got a squirt gun small enough to fit in the palm of my hand and loaded it with laundry bleach. I made several browsing (strafing) runs through the custom-clothing department, then left."

The Cheshire Cat said he could have worked faster if he'd taken two or three squirters into the store.

"Holy Halston, Batman, where'd you get those funky 501s? Levy me guess," I punned.

SWEETIES

Remember Joker from the IRS gig? Seems he wanted to have some additional fun with his former lady. Using a pencil, he carefully and lightly addressed an envelope to himself, stamped it, and mailed it.

While awaiting delivery, Joker wrote a fanciful sexual fantasy letter to his former sweetie from another one of his enemies, the male half of a troublesome couple from another neighborhood. In this letter, the secondary mark explained to ex-sweetie, the primary markess, how great it had been watching his wife and this ex-sweetie do oral sex to each other. He also wrote detailed descriptions of mixed anal sex, golden showers, and then got into some truly gross things.

"When my empty envelope arrived in the next day's mail, I very carefully erased my name, typed in my ex-sweetie's name as the addressee, then used the other couple for a return address. I carefully opened the envelope and popped in my sex fantasy letter," Joker explained.

The trigger for this trap was pulled when Joker

"accidentally" dropped this bogus letter in the women's bathroom of the business in which his ex-sweetie worked. Note use of past tense.

"George, you know human nature. The person who found that letter read it and probably either copied it or showed it to a whole bunch of other people before returning it to my ex," Joker related.

Joker reports that his markess left her job within two weeks.

◆

Steve Wilson tells me about a friend of his who was broken when his evil lady defected to some rich man who would buy her clothing and jewels. Steve's friend decided to get even.

He contacted Black Knight Leathers (see Sources) and ordered some kinky sex toys for his sweetie. He also included a handwritten note on some very studly stationery with the toys. The note read as follows:

Dear Sally,

Next time I'm in town, let's try these out. I know we've done about everything, and I know how bored you are at home, so I thought these toys and thoughts of my hard cock would make you all wet and ready for me. We'll be great together. We always are. I'll call.

Love,

Lars

Steve's pal waited until Sally, the ex-sweetie, was out of town on a business trip and her new sweetie was home alone. He had the parcel, addressed to both of them, delivered to their address. Sally's beau opened the package, found the note and the toys, then hit the ceiling. It's always much more fun if the guy's a prick, too. I have no after-action report from Steve or his friend. Let's assume the best.

◆

So, you get into an argument with sweetie and you want to get in some good put-downs, win the dozens, shortsheet the conjugal bed? Here are a few suggestions of come-backs and put-downs you can use. Some are gender-free, others have gender inclusions. If you're offended, joke you if you can't take a fuck!

- I should have listened to the guys/girls: you're a lousy fuck!
- Which smells worse, your breath, your farts, or your _____?
- Your face still looks like a boiled potato.
- Your breath (or some genital body part) smells like someone boiled a dead dog days ago.
- Sorry, I have a headache. By the way, have you had your vagina (or your choice of gendered parts) checked for radon?
- Is that your tongue, or are you wearing a used condom again?
- Do you have a younger brother (or sister)?
- If someone told you that you had to haul

your fat ass out of here you'd have to make three trips.
- Making love to you is like lying on a lumpy, sweaty pillow.
- My God, lady, it would take ten yards of wet cement to plug you.
- Geezus, you do more to contribute to male impotence than German measles.

TELEPHONES

Storm Trooper feels that a Hayduker's best friend may be a two-line conference call telephone. One of Storm Trooper's fun favorites is to conference his mark with the same nasty bully. Here's how he does it.

"I use line one to get the mark, while on the other phone, I am punching up the bully on line two. When I hear both lines ringing, I punch in the conference button on each phone and the fun starts," Storm Trooper says.

He cautions that you have to use two phones for this stunt, and you must punch the conference button on each. Storm Trooper adds that you must have two lines to make this work.

"Another twist is to call the bully and say, 'One moment, please, for the chief of police,' then switch to line two, call your mark, and press the conference button . . . same way to create fun," he adds.

You can make certain that both parties are available by ringing each before you connect them through conferencing.

Another suggestion is to conference two sweeties, especially if they happen to be married to other folks. Storm Trooper says a tape recording would be good here, especially if you wanted to send copies of the conversation to interested third parties—spouses, family, employers . . .

Storm Trooper told me that he once conferenced an abortion clinic with a prissy pro-life weasel. He also suggests getting two business or political competitors together, or ex-sweeties. The variations of this one are as unlimited as your imagination.

◆

Dick Smegma has a wonderfully useful imagination. He found a new use for Call Forwarding. Dick's idea is to Call Forward your mark's telephone to one in another country. You do this either by getting inside your mark's home or using a telephone serviceman's phone attached to the wire outside his home.

Try to hook your mark to a telephone that has a lot of traffic, such as a time/temperature phone or some tourist help line. Dick says this works best using phone numbers in Europe. The next step is to use someone else's phone, or a pay phone, to call the mark's number. Run a classified ad selling something so other people will call the number. This works well if the mark is away for a week or so.

Dick knew one person who programmed his mark's phone to ring in on a pay phone in

Germany in a large market area. He reports that the mark's telephone bill was astounding.

◆

There are many little known facts about available service that the various telephone companies don't want us to know. For example, The Wiz, who owns the Department of Unconventional Resources (see Sources), shares some interesting news. Your phone company charges your account if someone else makes an emergency interruption of your phone call. The Wiz says that if you use a pay phone you can run up some fun amounts on your mark's telephone bill by making emergency interruptions of his calls.

◆

My favorite Medic from Uncleland called to tell me how to make free phone calls using only a cassette recorder/player, an external speaker, an external microphone, a high-quality blank tape, and a trusted friend at a pay phone with about three dollars in change.

Your friend calls you at your pay-phone number. You lift the receiver and place the microphone, which is hooked to the recorder containing the tape, at the telephone's earpiece. Have your ally begin to slowly deposit the coins in the other phone. As you may or may not know, nickels, dimes, and quarters give different sounds when dropped into a coin slot. You now have these sounds on tape.

Dr. Medic says his friend demonstrated his tape by using the external speaker to replay the sound of the coins dropping when he dialed a long-distance number from yet another pay phone. It worked. For the record, he told me that a quarter is five rapid beeps, a dime is two, and a nickel is one.

He also said if it doesn't work the first time, adjust the volume up or down on your playback unit, and try again. I told Dr. Medic that this sort of thing was very illegal. He agreed and said that his friend did this only for experimental purposes and immediately destroyed the recording after it worked successfully several times.

◆

Speaking of telephone stuff, did you ever wonder where area code 800 is located? I've puzzled over that. Is it like lost Atlantis, some commercial American limbo-land? Do drones work there, or perhaps droids representing airlines, hotels, credit card companies, car rentals? Maybe it's all done by computer voices? Nah, I like the thought that it's a lost nation of people, now enslaved as reservation clerks, credit managers, telemarketing salespeople, and that ilk from the service industries.

Probably not. It's kind of silly, I guess. Just like my theory that the rings of Saturn are made up of lost airline luggage.

TELETHONS

What sort of depraved person would even consider making Jerry's Kids part of a nasty revenge scheme? That's actually a rhetorical question, as the answer lies in the fact that you're reading one of those sort of people's account of how another of that sort did use Jerry's Kids.

I refer to the Jerry Lewis Telethon, a television annual that's been around as long as the medium, it seems. Mike R. from L.A. had some trouble with a neighbor who was a mooch. The guy never "borrowed" anything big, just lots of little things and lots of little time, all of which added up to big. His return rate was nil.

"The guy was nuts about the Jerry Lewis Telethon," Mike related. "That's how we got back at him. We knew he watched most of it, so we went to my friend's house a few blocks away. The mark didn't know this friend, so we used his telephone.

"We called the telethon pledge number and used the mark's name for a $5,000 pledge with an unusual conditional request. We told the phone person that the pledge would be honored only if one of the guest celebrities would acknowledge it on the air with 'my' (actually, the mark's) name," Mike said.

Naturally, they wanted a call-back number. Mike said that his (the mark's) number was unlisted and please not to give it out or put it onto any sort of telemarketing computer or anything. Mike got the poor guy so concerned about this privacy thing that he totally forgot his suspicions about the number being whose Mike claimed it was.

Sure enough, five minutes later another person called back to verify the pledge, the name, and the request. Ten minutes later, another call came from a telethon official to verify. Mike's salesmanship did the trick again.

"I ran over to the mark's house and just kind of casually dropped in on him for a beer or two. We sat for a moment and watched the telethon, chatting. And, then it came on . . ."

Mike says Frankie Avalon came on the tube and said, "Hey, we want to thank Mr. _____ of _____, California, for his pledge of $5,000."

Mike also says the mark barfed his dinner right there on the floor, and that's no lie! What can you say about a guy who's willing to contribute his dinner (post-consumption) to Jerry's kids?

TELEVISION

Leave it to Joe from Washington to create a way to upset television reception for blocks on end. I don't know what set Joe off, but it must have been a bad-news neighbor. Anyway, here's Joe's plan.

Obtain an old-style, vibrating-type electric coil (one for the Model T Ford) from an auto supply shop. Attach a wire from the positive side of the coil to your own TV antenna. Ground the negative side of the coil with a wire to an iron pin in the ground.

Buy a six-volt dry cell at another shop. Wire the positive side of the battery to the positive side of the coil, and wire the negative side of the battery to the negative ground wire. When you have this connected properly, it will cause wavy lines and other interference on all TV sets within a two- to three-block radius.

If you wish to get sophisticated about it, you could wire a simple doorbell button into the system, connecting positive to positive and ground to ground, then pushing the button to activate the interference at will. Unpushed, no hassle with other folks' TV sets. Pushed? Hee, hee hee . . .

This is a lot of mojo power, my friends.

◆

Back again with more amazing stunts for your mark's TV, welcome Magic Z and his brother, Radioactive Waste, who will show you how to use a VCR rabbit, or remote, to disturb your mark's viewing. Our pals say you need to get the little infrared box from some source or other, the Homeboy Shopping Network or wherever. You then get into your mark's place and hook up the reception unit to his TV set, unless you know it's already prewired for the same.

The next step is to ruin TV viewing by activating your master remote in the direction of the receptor on the mark's set. You can change channels, turn the set off and on, or even key tapes if you've managed to sabotage/load the mark's VCR. Imagine if your mark has a kiddie's party in progress and you key up a porno flick!

This works great for next door or next apartment neighbors. If you get much further you will need a signal booster. A lot of stores sell them. Check it out.

◆

Ray Heffer spotted a fun device in a Johnson Smith catalog (see Sources). It's called a TV Oscillator, and the ad copy carries the warning that this device is *not* to be used as a TV jammer. Being the public-spirited citizen that he is, Ray wanted me to point that caution out to all of us.

Ray says there are also other sources for this educational device, some of which come in kit form. The application is that it will disrupt TV reception if it is used improperly by improper people. Imagine if some *improper* person went into a store that had irritated them and upset the television reception of all those dozens of mass TVs tuned to the same thing? Or, what if some *improper* person misused one of these in a bar?

Being proper people, Ray and I prey you won't misuse your unit.

TRASH

GI, penname for a truly diabolical friend, had a trash hauler who robbed him of badly needed sleep by his noiser-than-necessary handling of a Dumpster only twenty yards from GI's home. My friend works long, hard, and late; he needs his sleep. He asked the drivers for some consideration. Being mere crumbs at the base of the food chain, these cretins just stared dully at the sound of a human voice. He contacted the management of the hauling company and was told to accomplish an anatomically impossible sexual act. He contacted the nearby small company that owned the Dumpster. The boss there told GI that his fight was with the hauler, not him.

At this point, GI lost his patience but not his wit. He had noticed that the company owning the Dumpster had padlocked it, but that the haulers had a key. No problem. GI noted that the haulers always came on Friday morning at about 4:00. At 3:30, he put his own padlock on the Dumpster and waited. He heard no loud noise because the low-life haulers went away once they saw the second lock. GI immediately went out and removed his lock, and then he went to bed for some peaceful snoozing.

He did this for three weeks while all sorts of waste and trash piled up around the Dumpster. GI said he could just imagine the phone calls from the company to the haulers. Finally, after the third week, the boss from the neighboring company came over to ask GI if he knew anything about a mysterious second lock the haulers kept claiming was on the Dumpster when they arrived each week. GI looked at the boss and told him that his fight was with the haulers and not with him.

After the trick happened for the fourth week, the company moved the Dumpster to the other side of their plant, and GI was no longer bothered by noise. Happily, I told GI about this saying from the Koran, that there is more truth in one sword than in ten thousand words.

URINE

Alas, the hysterical idiocy over drugs and drug testing continues, as we give away more and more personal freedoms to our police-state masters. Thanks to some topical information from Dr. Catarrh L. Gingivitis, I can offer you some additional substitutes for your mandatory urine test. Several of the good doctor's suggestions follow.

• To raise the temperature of the sample, hold it under your armpit for a few minutes, or simmer in warm water for a few seconds.

• Substitute Diet Mountain Dew for your sample. This soft drink has the same pH and density as urine. Some say the taste is similar, also.

• According to a federal study, a copy of which Dr. Gingivitis sent me, despite its being classified, about 40 percent of all tests are faked. The margin of error in all tests is about 20 percent, despite government lies to the contrary.

The point is, if your pee fails its test for whatever reason, raise hell, act indignant, mention your barrister. After reading the government study and seeing how incompetent this whole program is, I suggest that you take advantage of the fact that too many kooks spoil the broth.

Am I against drug testing? Me? Of course not. Indeed, I am so cooperative that I will gladly submit to a urine test, right there, at that moment, on the spot, or, at least on the requester's shoes and/or hands.

UTILITY COMPANIES

A few years ago, Tony had a hassle with some neighborhood kids who shot at his house with a BB gun. He didn't know it, but they hit his electric meter box. He found out, he says, when he got a registered letter informing him that his power would be shut off unless he came into the utility company's office in person with a $350 security check and an explanation for his meter tampering.

Tony was flabbergasted. He says, "I'm a straight, nice guy, a family man in business. I have money, so what in hell would I tamper with my power meter for and risk getting electrocuted?"

When he went in, just slightly hot, he was met by an unctuous assistant manager we'll call Rodney. Rodney accused Tony of trying to steal electricity by meter tampering. He showed him the BB-damaged box and claimed Tony broke it by tampering. Tony explained he thought it was caused by neighbor kids, but he didn't really know for sure. He did know, for sure, that he had not done it. He also began to suspect that Rodney was not only a pompous asshole, but the true enemy in all of this.

Rodney's decision stood, and no amount of Tony's complaining up the line got anywhere. His attorney told him it would cost too much to sue and advised him to pay the fee, complain to the state public utility commission, then demand the fee back after a year of satisfactory payment.

"I agreed, but added one codicil of my own," Tony explained. "On my own, I found out where Rodney lived, then verified it. I waited a few months for all to calm down and for Rodney to take off for a weekend.

"That night I went to his place, broke the glass on his meter, and tampered with the wheels. Before I left, I noted the name of a nearby neighbor. I used that name and number to call the utility company's service department—not management where someone might know Rodney—and, pretending to be the neighbor, reported some funny sputtering of the power at Rodney's address."

Tony did nothing else until the year was up. Armed with his agreement he went into the power company office to get his refund. He asked for Rodney and was informed that Rodney no longer worked there. A new assistant manager, very nice by the way, gave him both a refund check and an apology.

VERMIN

Chester the Spoon once worked with a man whose thoughtfulness toward coworkers approached that of a garden slug. His intellect was very near to the weak link of the food chain. The man did have a vegetable garden, though, and it was about all he had of which he could be proud.

Chester recalled, "We tried to work this guy into normal society, but he remained a slug, until he got the bright idea that it would be cute to be the boss' snitch. Problem for him was that he wasn't smart enough to do it covertly. We passed along a few subtle warnings, which he ignored."

Chester had a pal, an old farm boy who remembered how miserable gardening was because of the pests who shared the garden, such as insects and furry things. Chester and his pal knew that sugar attracts insects and rancid animal fat draws vermin. They also knew about their mark's love for his garden.

They took squeeze bottles into Mr. Mark's garden one evening and doused the tops of plants with heavily sugared water and the lower areas with warm, liquid-rendered animal fat. The next move was for nature to take her coarse.

"It worked great. All the jerk could do at work was whine about the giant bugs munching his plants, and ask how come so many mice, rats, squirrels, and cats were fighting a war inside his garden area," Chester recalled with a smile.

Chester said one of the other workers told the mark to spray a mixture of Kool Aid and water over everything to get rid of the vermin. One other person said to mix some laundry bleach with water and spray that on the bug-ridden plants. Two weeks later, according to Chester, the man just did his job and didn't bother anyone anymore. I guess he was still in mourning for his garden. It had died.

VIDEO

Dick Smegma needed to get back at a video-rental outlet whose suckhead owner had done rotten to Dick's family in a very personal way. Here's what Dick thought about doing. He got a couple of truly explicit porno tapes, then had an associate rent two Disney-style kiddie tapes, using a secondary mark's name from the main mark's store.

Our hero fast-forwarded each kiddie tape to about the middle, stopped the machine, and took out the tape. He placed some electrical tape over that "hole" that prevents over- or re-recording over a pre-recorded tape, then replaced the kiddie tape in the one VCR.

He put his porno tape in the other VCR, selected an especially gross sequence, and recorded it onto the kiddie tape, using one VCR to feed and the other to record. He did this to both kiddie tapes.

He then rewound the two rental tapes and had his associate return them to the shop. Shortly, some family will rent one or two kiddie tapes, and the doctored one will be seen by a very unintended audience, parents of whom will cause some very serious shit for the store owner/mark. The secondary chaos this will create regarding inventory and other little time bombs will delight anyone interested in this use of paranoia as a revenge tactic.

VOMIT

As I've mentioned all along, vomit is very useful, both as a statement and as a substance. I am not alone in my admiration for this theatrical use of the contents of someone's stomach. For example, in his celebrated biography of Brigadier Sinden Pudd-Puller, written in 1789, Sir Alex Bristly Locust makes the observation that, "The very act of vomitus upon someone or something is the very soul of good humour and quite useful in calling attention to that wretch . . . Brigadier Pudd-Puller heartily recommended it as a gesture toward one's enemies."

Personally, I find it hilarious to vomit surreptitiously in your mark's fireplace or stove. Hopefully, it will have time to dry so that the smell is gone or at least abated until the stove or fireplace is lighted, because when that happens, the smell is something you can't quite imagine.

In an actual field test of this stunt, one of my associates in the Hayduke Institute for Semiology blew chunks on the wood stove of a certain mark in Kuhscheiss, Ohio. When Mr. Mark lighted the stove the following evening, the entire house had to be abandoned for three days of cleaning and airing.

XMAS

I figured since everyone else has taken the Christ out of Chri$tmas that I will, too. While a Christmas card is an economical substitute for a real present, it can also be a wonderful weapon in the mind of a creative Hayduker.

For example, Aunt Nancy—the personification of innocence, sweetness, and human kindness—thought it might be amusing for you to send Christmas cards to various people in your mark's name. The style, tone, and message of the card would, of course, be a matter of local and personal option, as would the specific recipients. I really like this idea. It's fraught with true mischief.

◆

Meanwhile, Mary Joan Michele found a fun way to deal with snooty, pushy shops and/or their clerks who pressure her during the holiday buying season. She says she buys most everything they suggest, even going into extravagant upgrades in gift selection. She naturally puts all of this on plastic so the snooty clerk/mark gets "credit" for the sale.

"For the next two days, I calmly do my real shopping, then late on the third day, I just as calmly return my purchases to the snooty/pushy store for credit, saying, 'After the very intense sales pressure from (mark's name) wore off, I found I really didn't need any of this. So sorry.'"

THE LAST WORD

Letters. That's the last word in this volume. Please write. I'm always glad to hear from readers and friends who have ideas, stunts, successes, plans, or funny stories they want to share. Send along questions, too, and I'll try to help in a general advisory way.

If you have something original and hilarious that you want me to use in a future book, please let me know in your letter.

I do personally answer all of my own mail, by the way. I try to be as prompt as possible in getting back to you, but I travel a lot, so please be patient.

Also, because I get such a huge volume of mail, I can't promise that you'll appear in my very next book. As before, please be patient with me.

One last thing, please include your name and return address with each letter, as I don't keep name and address files for friends. My address is:

George Hayduke
P.O. Box 1307
Boulder, CO 80306

Do Unto Others As They Have Done Unto You
With More Books By The Master of Mayhem!

With your purchase of this book, we welcome you to the Hayduke family!

And if you like this book, you'll love the other books by George Hayduke, the master of mayhem. Hayduke's arsenal of humorous ideas shows you how to handle all the punks and jerks you encounter everyday. If you've got one book, you'll need them all!

Ask for these titles at your bookstore. Or to order direct from the publisher call 1-800-447-BOOK (MasterCard or Visa) or send a check or money order for the books purchased (plus $3.00 shipping and handling for the first book ordered and 50¢ for each additional book) to Carol Publishing Group, 120 Enterprise Avenue, Dept. 569, Secaucus, NJ 07094.

The Complete Works of Hayduke, Available Through Carol Publishing Group

Advanced Backstabbing and Mudslinging Techniques
paperback $7.95 (#40560)

Getting Even: The Complete Book of Dirty Tricks
oversized paperback $12.95 (#40314)

Getting Even 2
oversized paperback $12.95 (#40337)

Make 'em Pay: Ultimate Revenge Techniques from the Master Trickster
paperback $7.95 (#40421)

Make My Day: Hayduke's Best Revenge Techniques for the Punks in Your Life
paperback $7.95 (#40464)

Mayhem: More From the Master of Malice
paperback $7.95 (#40565)

Revenge: Don't Get Mad, Get Even
oversized paperback $14.95 (#40353).

Righteous Revenge: Getting Down to Getting Even
paperback $8.95 (#40569)

NOTE: The dirty tricks presented in these books were created for entertainment purposes only. They are not for children or the mentally unbalanced.

Prices subject to change; books subject to availability